JAZ AMPAW-FARR

Because of You, This is Me

THE STORIES WE TELL, THE STORIES WE CHANGE AND THE POWER OF EVERYDAY HEROES

independent thinking press

First published by

Independent Thinking Press
Crown Buildings, Bancyfelin, Carmarthen, Wales, SA33 5ND, UK
www.independentthinkingpress.com

and

Independent Thinking Press
PO Box 2223, Williston, VT 05495, USA
www.crownhousepublishing.com

Independent Thinking Press is an imprint of Crown House Publishing Ltd.

© Jaz Ampaw-Farr, 2025

The right of Jaz Ampaw-Farr to be identified as the author of this work has been asserted by her in accordance with the Copyright, Designs and Patents Act 1988.

First published 2025, reprinted 2026.

All rights reserved. Except as permitted under current legislation no part of this work may be photocopied, stored in a retrieval system, published, performed in public, adapted, broadcast, transmitted, recorded or reproduced in any form or by any means, without the prior permission of the copyright owners. Enquiries should be addressed to Independent Thinking Press.

Independent Thinking Press has no responsibility for the persistence or accuracy of URLs for external or third-party websites referred to in this publication, and does not guarantee that any content on such websites is, or will remain, accurate or appropriate.

Edited by Ian Gilbert.

EU GPSR Authorised Representative
Appointed EU Representative: Easy Access System Europe Oü, 16879218
Address: Mustamäe tee 50, 10621, Tallinn, Estonia
Contact Details: gpsr.requests@easproject.com, +358 40 500 3575

British Library Cataloguing-in-Publication Data
A catalogue entry for this book is available from the British Library.

Print ISBN 978-178135298-4
Mobi ISBN 978-178135320-2
ePub ISBN 978-178135321-9
ePDF ISBN 978-178135322-6

LCCN 2025931343

Printed and bound in the UK by
CPI Antony Rowe, Chippenham, Wiltshire

Praise for *Because of You, This is Me*

An incredibly powerful book. Deeply moving yet inspirational, deeply personal yet incisive in its analysis of the education sector. More than anything, it provides a voice and an insight into the lives of children in classrooms that are often unseen and misunderstood by educators and policy makers. An essential read.

Professor Damien Page, Vice Chancellor, Buckinghamshire New University

Because of You, This is Me is more than a memoir, it's a masterclass in resilience, courage and the power of human connection. Jaz Ampaw-Farr's raw honesty, humour and unwavering determination leap off the page. Her story, rooted in childhood trauma, is heartbreaking, yet it's also an inspiring testament to the transformative power of small acts of kindness. This book is a love letter to the everyday heroes – teachers, mentors and friends – who saw past her circumstances and helped her build a different future. It's impossible to read this without reflecting on our own power to impact others. A must-read for anyone who believes in the strength of the human spirit.

Zara Janjua, presenter, journalist and writer

Jaz Ampaw-Farr's book is shocking, searing, moving and enraging yet ultimately uplifting. All the right feelings we should be feeling when confronted by a story as powerful and as honestly told as this. Jaz's USP is her honesty, her refusal to bend the truth so it can be palatable or 'presented', and this is why her work always leads us by the gut, galvanising us not to tolerate what is unfair, unequal and disrespectful, and to gather the courage to call out the unacceptable. The heroes in her world are teachers and not just because hers helped her, but because she recognises and celebrates the fact that a teacher has the most important job in the whole world: encouraging, nurturing and architecting the next generation.

Leslee Udwin, BAFTA multi-award-winning producer/director, human rights campaigner, founder and executive chair at Think Equal

Because of You, This is Me by Jaz Ampaw-Farr is one of the most inspiring, wonderful and informative books I have read in a long time. Jaz's openness and authenticity shine through as she bravely shares her story, taking us from the depths of despair in her upbringing to the remarkable person she is today. Her journey is nothing short of courageous, and it's a testament to the resilience of the human spirit.

The narrative is a heartfelt love letter to the teachers who have shaped her life and career. Jaz reflects on her past with a raw honesty that is both touching and enlightening. Rather than succumbing to the pain and heartache of her childhood, she transforms these struggles into powerful lessons of hope and strength. This remarkable ability to turn adversity into inspiration is what makes her story resonate so deeply.

Throughout the book, readers will laugh, cry and find themselves reflecting on their own experiences. Jaz's journey encourages us to look at our own lives with a new perspective, reminding us that our past does not define us but rather moulds us into who we can become.

I cannot recommend this book enough. It is a beautiful piece of writing that will linger in your heart and mind long after you've turned the last page. If you're seeking inspiration and a reminder of the power of resilience, *Because of You, This is Me* is a must-read.

Gemma Oaten, actress, TV and radio presenter, CEO of SEED

Contents

Author's Note .... *iii*
Acknowledgements .... *v*
Introduction 1

Mrs Cook 5
The One Who Taught Me Bravery

Mr Williams 35
The One Who Taught Me Truth

Mr Simpson 63
The One Who Taught Me Consistency

Miss Archer 95
The One Who Taught Me Audacity

Mr Readman 117
The One Who Taught Me Compassion

The Power of Everyday Heroes 141
Last Words 147
Courageous Conversations 151
Letter to the Eight-Year-Old Me 155
To the Survivors Reading These Words 157
References 159
About the Author 161
Let's Chat 163

Author's Note

This is my lived experience.

It's not the whole story – just the part I'm ready to tell. The part that demanded to be written.

Some names have been changed. Some scenes are stitched together for clarity. Nothing I describe is fiction.

Memory is strange. Some moments live in technicolour. Others are gone, swallowed whole. But this is what I remember.

If you're in this book, know that I wrote with love. If you're missing from these pages, it doesn't mean you didn't make a mark. Some things are too painful, too private, or too precious to fit between two covers.

This isn't a book about blame. It's a book about impact.

It's about how one seemingly small act can interrupt a trajectory and transform a life. It's about you.

Acknowledgements

Actual Acknowledgements

The bit where I try to thank a stadium's worth of people in the space of a few lines. On the flip side, this also doubles up as my Oscars speech and eulogy!

Writing this book has been like emotionally crowd-surfing through my own past – chaotic, a bit sweaty and with occasionally painful elbow pokes. Ultimately, it's all been worth it and was made possible by a fantastic army of humans who showed up, stood with me and carried me all the way through to writing this page of thanks. Whilst it appears at the front of the book, it's one of the last things I wrote.

To Ed

You've loved every version of me since that day I won you in a competition! From the 'off the shizang with creative energy' version to the 3am snot-snivelled, 'I'm crap at this writing lark and this book will never be finished' version! Thank you for holding me when I fall and reminding me (again and again) that it's okay to be me.

To Our Kids

You continue to bring me more joy than it's possible for my heart to hold. Thank you for allowing me to parent you while still learning how to reparent myself. You are who I want to be when I grow up.

To My Fabulous Family
(my chosen ones and the OGs)

I'm aware that life with me has been a rollercoaster! Thank you for being my inner circle and standing with me through thick, thin and medium rare. You keep me grounded.

Strap yourselves in for the next chapter!

To Team Jaz

You are my backstage glitter glue! Without you, there would be no frontstage. Zero. Zilch. Thank you for your ridiculous talent and expertise behind the scenes that allows me to simply show up and shine.

To My BOYTIM Team

Your infinite patience and encouragement have been above and beyond what any publisher should have to withstand! Thank you for reassuring me, more than anyone else, that my story matters, for helping me to find my voice in print and for the complete absence of semi-colons in this book.

To <u>All</u> Everyday Heroes

Whatever your role, this entire book is a love letter to you. Thank you for standing against the tide and paving a way for kids like me to be more than their postcode, their difference or their trauma. Your compassion creates generational legacy. Oh, and stop inserting the word 'just' before your job title. Your work changes lives!

To <u>My</u> Everyday Heroes

Thank you for seeing behind my front. For being human first and teacher second. For standing for and with me while I did everything to push you away. My heart aches with gratitude. Everything I am and everything I have is because of you.

To You, Who Found Something Familiar in These Pages

Thank you for sticking with me. If any part of my story resonates with any part of your story, know this: you are not alone. You are not broken. It is not too late. Reach out today. The pen is in your hand.

And finally ...

To the Little Girl Crouched in the Cellar

You made it, little one. You wrote your truth on the inside of your mind. You navigated every barrier and came back from every defeat. You did the work and together we turned pain into purpose. Mess became magic, then a keynote, then a book, and now a movement.

Because of you, this is me.

Aspirational Acknowledgements

These are people I've never met but have played a major part in me being brave enough to even start writing this book. Bypass me and check them out for your own 10% braver journey!

June Sarpong, OBE – for unapologetically showing up, taking up and creating space for other voices.

Brené Brown – for rebranding vulnerability and creating a game-changing shift from shame.

Oprah Winfrey – for being a constant trailblazer and driving force behind me believing that my past is not a script for my future.

Viola Davis – for a life lived and a memoir that makes the hairs on the back of your neck stand to attention. (Your book is the reason I didn't give up on writing mine.)

Trevor Noah – for being a recklessly generous, professionally vulnerable, personally authentic and honest storyteller.

Sir Ken Robinson – for consistently calling education up.

Queen Bey – for being you, meaning I'm able to run a nice side hustle as a pound shop Beyoncé lookalike!

My best

Jaz

(Mic drop. Exit stage left. Collapse on the sofa with a packet of chocolate Hobnobs and a large mojito!)

Introduction

The call came just after midnight.

On the same day I was booked to do seventeen TV and radio interviews promoting BBC's *The Apprentice*, I had to go and identify my little brother's body.

Paul had died alone. On the floor of a squat. Heroin overdose.

The phone call informing me of Paul's passing shattered my carefully constructed world. Instead of a week spent prancing around as a glitzy Z-list reality TV star, being a great sport as celebs made jokes about my first-week firing, I headed for my hometown. It was a place I'd avoided for years. Too many memories and a stark reminder of the truth I knew – I was a fraud.

Twenty-four hours after collapsing on my kitchen floor in grief and guilt, I stood outside the hospital. The same hospital Paul and I had been taken to on the first of several occasions when we were removed from our parents and placed into foster care. Still wearing the same outfit I'd worn in Lord Sugar's boardroom, I walked down the corridor looking like a successful adult but feeling like a broken child.

Paul and I shared more than DNA. I was more than Paul's big sister. I was his protector. We lived in a squat but inside my mind I was a knight trying to keep her four-year-old charge safe by standing in between him and danger. I'd failed. To unpick how I went on to survive, thrive, be truly alive we need to step back into the shadows of our shared past.

I wrote this book while locked in a cellar.

Crouching on damp stairs in the darkness was frightening but familiar.

I thought I was clever back then, developing what seemed like the perfect survival strategy – wrapping my arms around my bare knees, making myself as small as possible so as to avoid any other part of my body coming into contact with the wet brick stairs. My feet would shuffle from side to side, serving two critical purposes: fighting off the numbness from the freezing cold and scaring away the rats.

Pretty innovative plan for a seven-year-old.

My parents didn't think I was that clever. In their words, I was a defiant, gobby, spiteful, f*cking useless, black b*tch whore and filthy n*gger. I didn't understand half the names they called me, but the venomous and angry way those words were spat at me left me in no doubt of the hate I seemed to provoke.

What I didn't understand was why. I invested countless hours trying to work out exactly what I said or did to cause their intense dislike of me. Even when I tried to be 'good' it made zero difference. The only thing I knew for sure was that none of it was fair.

Despite a strong and constant sense of injustice, I tried to accept my fate. I repeatedly struggled to keep my face from screwing up into a scowl when they shouted and screamed at me. Instead, I forced myself to nod in vigorous agreement with their words, hoping it would show that I accepted and believed I deserved everything I got. It never once worked. The lie was so big it made me physically sick to tell it.

Answering back guaranteed a day in the cellar – sometimes a night as well if they forgot to let me out before going to the pub – so I made the time go quicker by channelling my physical pain, intense fear and the promise from my stepfather that he would one day kill me and throw my broken body down the very stairs I was crouched on into writing a book.

This book.

Back then the title was '*The Truth According To Me*'. It was an indignant girl's attempt to explain to her world of teachers, social workers and other well-meaning adults why it was too big a risk to trust them.

I knew exactly how the book should be. Not in the least bit shouty or cross. I had already learned adults saw that as 'challenging behaviour' and were more likely to respond with a 'good talking to' than the 'good listening to' I needed. No, this book was going to be honest and it was going to be kind. It was going to describe clearly and patiently the gap that existed between people's understanding of what happened at home and what happened at school. It would outline what I needed and explain the exact steps in how to connect, engage and enrol me. Everyone would read it. Everyone would understand it. Everyone would make sure that what was happening to me would never happen to any other seven-year-old.

This book is an evolution of that book. It celebrates the five Everyday Heroes (and a cast of accidental saviours) who reached into the darkness and pulled me towards the light through seemingly small but transformative actions. While

Paul and I shared the same chaotic childhood at home, at school I had something he lacked: adults who made me feel like I belonged, who saw my worth, who refused to give up on me even when I'd given up on myself.

In the pages you're about to read, I've tried to answer the question that haunted me as I stood in that hospital corridor trying to force my feet to move forward: how does a child survive when the system fails? The answer includes the story of how a broken little girl blazes into a woman with a habit of being 10% braver. But more than that, it's a love letter acknowledging and shining a light on the extraordinary power of ordinary humans – in my case, five teachers who went beyond the curriculum to transform lives through seemingly small but profound acts of human connection.

I've attempted to describe exactly how these Everyday Heroes saw past my behaviour to my potential. How they met me where I was rather than where they needed me to be. How they stood shoulder to shoulder with me in the chaotic fire that was my life and refused to move, even when I pushed them away. In short, they were human first and professional second. There's no getting away from it, some of what I describe makes for a harrowing read. If you find it particularly difficult because it reminds you of experiences you've had yourself, please stay with me. I want to show you what it looks like on the other side of healing.

The book you're reading now isn't quite the one I imagined back then. Paul's death may have been the catalyst for this but it's my best attempt at a thank you. To the Everyday Heroes who changed, saved and totally transformed my life through seemingly small but highly impactful actions. It's an encouragement to anyone navigating chaos and ready to be 10% braver themselves. It's your roadmap for change.

And if you lead or work with children or young people in any sense, the answer to how I survived, thrived, drove change and became truly alive is simple:

Because of you.

Mrs Cook
The One Who Taught Me Bravery

There she stood. Older, yet styled in the same unmistakable 1970s vibe. Still wearing brown.

I had returned to my old primary school, now on my way to becoming a teacher myself, to find my first teacher. Mrs Cook. The one who has set me on my current path. The one who had taught me to fear less. The one who had unknowingly saved my *actual* life.

I had returned to tell her that I was finally on my way to fulfilling her prophecy and becoming a teacher myself. My heart started to race as I approached her in the playground, watching her comfort a crying boy with the same gentle encouragement I remembered being on the receiving end of. My legs felt like jelly. It was as if I was about to meet Beyoncé herself!

I'd been in the same state as that boy and, for a moment, I remembered the familiar taste of despair mixed with distress that I'd often turned up in at school. I arrived in many classrooms already broken. I was a nervous child without the words to describe what was happening when I wasn't in the safety of my school buildings. But Mrs Cook had a way of making every child feel seen, by converting fear into bravery.

I called her name, she turned and … brace yourself for the big reveal … I don't think she even remembered me!

Of course, that didn't matter. As soon as she saw me, she smiled that same sparkling smile and I was transported to being six years old again, off to retrieve my book from my tray so I could stand at her desk and read! I was overcome with the same complete and utter belonging I felt in her presence all those years ago. That smile was the smile that I'd seen in my mind's eye when, aged eleven, I had summoned the necessary bravery to escape the pimp I'd ended up living with.

I fought back the tears as I explained who I was and tried to describe the monumental impact on my life whilst being mindful that she was on break duty in my old school playground surrounded by several dishevelled six-year-olds, hot and sweaty from running around outside on a hot day.

Mrs Cook placed her hand on my arm, just like she used to when I was one of her 'ladies and gentlemen' in her Rainbow Class, and a feeling of overwhelming love surged through my body.

Mrs Cook: 'You're doing well?'

Me (*unsuccessfully fighting back sobs*): 'Yes, I'm going to be a teacher, just like you said.'

Mrs Cook: 'I am *so* proud of you.'

Proud of me.

Recalling this moment and writing it for you makes the hairs on the back of my neck stand up. There's just no way that I could capture the full weight of that moment in a couple of paragraphs. Let me tell you how I got here. How one teacher, forever styled in brown, taught me how to be 10% braver.

The power of being seen

Mrs Cook was my first teacher. A true style queen whose whole wardrobe came in chocolate brown. Every day there was a different combination of chocolate brown smocks over chocolate brown turtleneck sweaters with chocolate brown tights and chocolate brown buckled shoes. Her warm smile and shining hazel eyes gave her the air of a children's TV presenter. She was softly spoken and quick to laugh. I don't remember her ever raising her voice, which was light and sparkly. When she read stories, it was like being wrapped in a cuddly blanket. Just being around Mrs Cook made you happy.

Besides being my teacher, Mrs Cook was the first Everyday Hero I ever met. She (literally) saved my life, but, like the other Everyday Heroes I'll be introducing you to in this book, she never knew it.

Mrs Cook's classroom reflected her personality (except with a more adventurous colour palette). It was a warm, psychedelic pink and blue safe extension of herself in which we could all flourish. She made it 'our' space, whether she was in the room or not, and it was always full of interesting things to discover and cocooned corners to reset. The classroom I went on to set up as a teacher was directly modelled on the environment she created that made school feel like the home I dreamed of having.

In Mrs Cook's class, there were no pupils. She referred to us as 'ladies and gentlemen of Rainbow Class'. We were her 'authors' and 'inventors', and she encouraged – well, insisted on – our learning through making and celebrating our mistakes, knowing it would embed ambitious resilience or whatever it was called back then.[1] There was no question that she loved every one of us. In fact, I had a sneaky suspicion that I was her favourite – although she made every child lucky enough to come into contact with her feel like that. Many of my classmates also believed that they were her favourite.[2]

Mrs Cook had a way of making every child feel seen. When the fire alarm test was due, she'd quietly call me to her desk before it went off. Making reassuring eye contact with me, she'd hold my hand. A small act of kindness that meant so much to me I still vividly remember it today.

Thanks to Mrs Cook, I fell in love with learning. Her teaching provided so many adventures to get stuck into that school was a haven of hyperfocus. I spent hours on tasks and frequently became lost in an activity. For me, it was the transition out of those moments of bliss that I found challenging. They required me to 'just be', and I had no baseline for that. I needed a focus to pour myself into and disliked too many choices. My classmates enjoyed the freedom of choice. The same freedom that to me felt like chaos. My head was a 24/7 whirl of ideas and creativity, but with no map to guide me, I bit my nails, cried at the suggestion of any change to the routines of the school day and jumped at the slightest unfamiliar sound.

Mrs Cook sensed my discomfort and, aware that the last fire drill had resulted in me wetting myself in fear, she made sure to call me up to her desk to read the next time one was planned. She squeezed my hand and maintained eye contact just before it was due to start, to reassure me without alerting my friends that I was terrified and sparing me any embarrassment. I'm still grateful for that intuition and kindness – and not just when there was a fake fire.

Back then, I was far from brave. Anxiety was a familiar and constant companion even before I was plunged into a world of violence and criminality. As an adult, a doctor once advised me that the simple lack of nurturing physical

---

1 I think it was just called 'learning'.
2 They were wrong. It was me.

contact from my mother in my early years created a level of fear and uncertainty that my little girl brain would never be able to heal from. I thought it best not to freak him out, so opted not to fill him in on what happened after I left Mrs Cook's class.

What's Love Got To Do With It?

For as long as I can remember, I've thought in pictures then wrapped words around them to explain my thoughts to someone else. It turns out I was an expert in metaphors before I knew what a metaphor was. I'd remember events in technicolour as if they were scenes from a film I'd replayed countless times in my mind. This resulted in me creating alternative worlds in my mind, in order to make sense of the one I was fighting to exist in.

I was six years old when I realised love came in different flavours. From the multi-faceted and alluring minty choccy chip to gloriously standard vanilla. All humans were ice-creams. On my part, I loved my nan, grandad and Mrs Cook back, but had zero warm fuzzy feelings for Paul – my new baby brother. He was an impractically small human whose only talents appeared to be crying, pooping and distracting my nan from looking after me.

My nan's love was practical, and her sole purpose in life seemed to be to defeat the evil of cold weather. Consumed with the prevention of anyone catching a chill, her love was delivered out in short sharp soundbites like 'N'ere cast a clout till May be out' that made you feel you should have disposed of something by June but were unsure exactly what it was!

Generous with her love, she offered everyone a slice of weathered wisdom, whether they asked for it or not. This embarrassingly included random passers-by dressed in outfits that indicated a clear lack of planning and rendered them woefully unprepared for the forthcoming ice age. In the gospel according to my nan, not tucking your vest into your pants was a crime roughly on par with bank robbery.

Nan was tall and strong with Dame Edna-style glasses that dangled on a chain around her neck. She made sure my baby brother and I had what we needed: food, clothes, a bed and a roof over our heads. I loved the simplicity of her black-and-white view of the world, even when it didn't make sense. She busied herself with being one who works hard and 'speaks as I find'. I loved her no-nonsense straight talk – except for when that involved telling me or my grandad off. Then, not so much.

I loved how my nan kept a not-so-secret stash of rich tea biscuits in a battered tin under her pile of knitting and would sneak one to me with a sharp tap on the shoulder while I sat at her feet waiting for the latest addition to my raglan cardi collection to be finished. I loved how she devoured the Mills and Boon romantic novels she bought from the outdoor market, getting a little flustered and muttering 'Bleddi 'ell' every now and again. I loved bedtime with my nan, which meant being tucked in the top bunk so tight you could hardly move. It was a nightly race to fall asleep before your arms went numb.

It was my nan who stepped up and took care of me when my biological mother showed disinterest in doing so. It was my nan who claimed the 'little brown baby' left in a pram outside a pub for several hours on a cold winter night. It was my nan who stayed by the side of my hospital cot while I battled the bout of pneumonia that followed and nursed me back to health over the next few months. Most of all, I loved that my nan never let me miss a day of school, taking charge of the school run after the latest in the long line of 'uncles' my biological mother had sent to collect me went missing in action.

Nan's ongoing battle with 'the cold' was a success. She made me feel warm, both physically and emotionally.

My grandad's love was constantly present and connected. After school, I'd sit with my nose pressed up against the glass of the front room bay window to get the first glimpse of him walking around the corner from the bus stop. By the time his key was in the lock, I'd be at the door, squealing with excitement, ready to start our evening routine of wrapping my arms around one of his oil and grease-stained trouser legs and sitting on one of his steel-capped boots as he dragged me along with ease asking my nan where I was!

He didn't get a break from me at dinner time and was happy for me to sit on the arm of his favourite threadbare chair while he ate the meat and two veg dinner my nan had kept warm for him under the grill. He always pretended not to notice as I sneakily dipped my thumb in the congealed gravy around the edge of his plate.

I loved the smell of his ever-present Polo mints mingled with the rich liquorice odour of tobacco and the way he made me repeatedly promise that I would never smoke a pipe. I loved the way he tittered while we watched *Morcambe and Wise* on TV at the weekend and the way he squeezed my hand and whispered 'Try using more of that Brylcreem, love' to my nan as I screamed in pain while she attempted to guide her old white-lady comb through my reluctant-to-be-tamed Afro hair.

My grandad never got cross, apart from the time I stumbled into the bathroom when he was getting out of the bath, and he covered himself with a towel, shouting at me to get out. 'Some parts of our body ...' he explained afterwards by way of an apology, '... are private. They're not for showing to other people.' I later learned that not every adult who came into my life felt the same way.

Grandad told me stories and made me memorise the Lord's Prayer with all the 'thys' and 'trespasses' (hard to remember and even harder to say when your two front teeth are missing) and instilled in me a sense of fairness and integrity. He stressed the importance of 'doing the right thing' and referenced his time in the army during World War Two. It was clear that the experience had clearly cost him, transforming him from the tall, handsome, happy and now almost unrecognisable young fella in the black-and-white photo on nan's dresser.

As I watched his health deteriorate, a lifetime of smoking – man and boy – taking its toll, the mood in the house changed. I couldn't explain it in words, but, ever sensitive to the countenance of the adults around me, I knew that I was losing something I would never get back. My grandad never got to see my seventh birthday.

Then there was Mrs Cook. Her love was on a whole different level and unlike anything I'd experienced in my short life. She wasn't related to me and had no obligation to love me and that made it all the more impactful. This was a different flavour of love – fun, sparkly (like her eyes) and firmly future-focused. Mrs Cook was enthralled about the exciting things we would go on to do and had every student enthralled too. She came from a place of unshakeable certainty that every one of us had the capacity to be fantastic adults. She expected nothing less, and the last thing I wanted to do was to let her down.

She had a way of making you feel like you could do the impossible. She used to ask us, '*Who* are you going to *be* when you grow up?' Not '*What* are you going to *do*?' How powerful is that question – who are you going to be?[3]

The class heartthrob slightly embarrassed himself by shouting out 'I wanna be a daddy!' The rest of us broke out into laughter, but not Mrs Cook. She told us to protect our dreams, no matter how many people ridiculed them. When the gods of registration order dictated that it was my turn to speak up, I really wanted to get the answer right. The only problem was that I had no clue what the answer was. My 'mindset poverty' was already starting to consolidate, and

---

3 It's a great question for today. In a world where human connection is a currency and half the jobs seven-year-olds will go on to do haven't even been invented yet.

anything beyond surviving the next day seemed too audacious to dream of. I looked at her with a blank expression on my face, masking the summersault circus of turmoil and panic inside my mind and forcing my thoughts into silent movies, just like I'd practised at home. Mrs Cook just smiled and confidently waited for an answer.

That's when it came. The truth. I blurted out, 'I want to be just like you!' My classmates roared with laughter. I immediately felt embarrassed, stupid and, well, wrong. It scared me because that level of panic was a feeling I hadn't experienced before in the safe haven that was Mrs Cook's classroom. My heartbeat quickened but Mrs Cook didn't flinch. She looked straight back at me and asked/told me in a clear, kind but firm tone, 'You mean you want to be a teacher?'

I recognised the words she spoke as belonging to the English language but wasn't able to comprehend, let alone process, what she had just said. A teacher? Had she lost her mind? People like me don't grow up to be teachers. Even if I was a good enough human (which I wasn't), there was one obvious problem.

Teachers. Aren't. Brown.

I'd internalised information from my surroundings so deeply they became facts. My world was pretty much exclusively white and included a large contingent of people inside and outside of my family who were unafraid to speak their minds about their perceived lack of value attached to my skin colour. The only brown adult I'd seen in school was the lady with the lovely lilac Afro who came in to hoover the glitter from the carpet as we left for home. Representation wasn't lacking – it was non-existent.

Everyone in my family was white and the only other person I'd seen with my skin colour was the children's TV presenter Derek Griffiths, who I spent my early years assuming was my actual dad (while secretly praying that Floella Benjamin was my real mum). It wasn't difficult to overhear my nan's friends advise of the shame associated with having a granddaughter who was a 'filthy half-breed' as they weren't 'backwards in coming forward', as my nan would say, with their opinions. Nan never responded to them and silently dismissed what she described as 'silly boggers' but she did start letting go of my hand and telling me to walk behind her when we went past certain shops. So yeah, the idea of teachers (aka the best adults to walk the planet) being brown was way outside of what I could consider plausible. Unconsciously, I'd drawn the conclusion and accepted that people like me weren't allowed to do things like that. If anyone told me anything different, I hadn't heard them.

Mrs Cook's statement presented a huge problem. I believed and trusted her even though it felt like lying. I looked down at my knees and bit my bottom lip, buying time and trying to conjure up a more realistic movie franchise in my mind. Mrs Cook was having none of it. She pressed on and sealed the deal by bolstering my bravery with her next statement. With a relaxed certainty in her voice, she asserted, 'That's a great idea because *you* are going to make a *fantastic teacher*!'

Not just a teacher – a 'fantastic' one!

Her statement had the ring of a fairytale to it and my scepticism gave way to worry as I realised the one thing that stood in the way of this amazing dream:

I didn't own enough brown clothes to pull that off!

Nevertheless, it was decided. Mrs Cook drove a stake into the ground that was my unknown future, attached a piece of elastic to it and tied the other end around my waist to be sure. Simple as that. She believed that every child who arrived in her class was gifted and talented and it was her job to uncover what those gifts and talents were. If she had spotted the inner teacher in me, then my job was to make it happen and prove her confidence in me was well founded. I knew my nan only knitted clothes in navy wool, so there was only one course of action I could take – I immediately started collecting toilet rolls and egg boxes. After all, one of the defining factors of teachers seemed to be that they had an endless supply of both.[4]

The strongest memories I have of Mrs Cook's love involved asserting how brave I was and finding ways to reward me for that bravery. I didn't feel brave, but she painted me in a colour that I didn't have in my palette. She gave me new bright colours and encouraged me to use them in paintings that spoke of a world outside of my own garden of possibility. Looking at a paintbox of familiar grey and choosing to dip your brush in an audacious bright yellow takes bravery. That's what she taught me. To use that bright yellow bravery to paint safety and stability.

---

4   I collected these for years, although later I would get into trouble in one foster home for unravelling whole rolls of toilet paper and hiding the evidence under my bed. The 'theft and vandalism', as one of my adults called it, was actually an attempt at soothing myself when I felt scared. My plan was to collect enough empty tubes until I finally had enough to run away, prove that I was an acceptable human and become a teacher. I still struggle to simply chuck a toilet roll tube in the recycling today!

Jazanory!

The only thing Mrs Cook and I disagreed on was the book *Where The Wild Things Are* by Maurice Sendak. She loved it, and I hated it. The muted colours, the wild things being too scary, even Max gave me the pip! It looked like one long argument with sulking at the end, which was far too close to my home life for me to enjoy a book about it in school. I'd go on to intensely dislike the Enid Blyton books I was encouraged to read in school later. Picnicking middle-class white children who had parents who loved them and spent their days having adventures in fields felt too far-fetched to me.

Roald Dahl was also problematic as the stories had cruel adults front and centre. Bear with me here, because I know these stories are beloved and for good reason. However, as a child, the neglect and abuse of Matilda was kind of triggering, only not as a memory from the past but as my current reality at home. I found it too close to my actual experience and felt stupid for not being able to enjoy the stories like my friends seemed to. I assumed everyone was experiencing the same things as me, but I was rubbish at pushing it down. It left me feeling genuinely confused as to why I was expected to read and enjoy books that depicted similar treatment to what I was being subjected to at home.

One of Mrs Cook's strategies for increasing our confidence was to encourage us to use the stories she had read as springboard inspiration for our own. This included zero focus on the incessant use of semi-colons.[5] Listening to Mrs Cook read a story was like living the adventure. She would help us become lost in the narrative, and then, after reading, she would ask great questions that gave us permission to retrace our steps to expand the story even more.

It was because of this that I told her I would no longer be taking part in any 'Wild Things' related activities! Looking back, it was a testament to the culture she created in our class that allowed me to speak out. When she asked me what I didn't like about the story, all I could come up with was that, in some way, I felt that the story was 'broken'. She just smiled her usual smile and suggested I write one that wasn't.

I was, she reminded me, already an experienced author. Encouraged by the contained freedom she created for me, I knew exactly what I would write about.

Her.

---

[5] Mrs Cook wasn't a rogue revolutionary. This was pre national curriculum. Also, I manage to reach the ripe old age of forty without ever needing to use a semi-colon, so go figure.

Mrs Cook was always sharing little snippets from her life outside the classroom. For example, we all knew she loved daisies, lived at the bottom of a hill and had a husband called 'Mr Cook'. All the important stuff. One winter's day, when it was icy, she told us how she had left Mr Cook trying to drive up the hill and had walked to school instead. At that moment, I had the quite frankly hilarious notion of writing about her husband in his car on an icy hill.

From the second I came up with that idea, I couldn't stop smiling. I was about to do something that would amaze and delight my teacher. What's more, I already knew I was a literary genius – Mrs Cook had said so. I knew that all I needed to do was set about writing this bestselling work of comedy gold. However, there was just one problem – I didn't fully understand how writing worked.

Reading wasn't a problem. My grandad had taught me how to attach phonemes to graphemes and blend words. I memorised the words that didn't play by the rules and, as a result, smashed the Schonell Reading Test. My reward was the prestige of being a red table reader. The obstacle I was up against was that I had no idea how this process worked in reverse. Of course, Mrs Cook was always on hand to help, but this was one story I wanted to do all by myself.

Undaunted, I put pencil to paper, trying to work out what letters I needed. When I got stuck, I asked around for help. I became consumed with this and went as far as asking different friends how to write different words. That way, no one could guess the full story, steal my idea and become a bestselling author on the back of my toil! I spent several days in stealth mode, and it was a slow process. In the evenings, I asked my nan and grandad how to write certain words at home and snuck them in on crumpled pieces of paper to copy into my book. I was engaged, persistent, a little obsessed and determined to finish. I enjoyed feeling like I was on an important mission that, once complete, would change the world – well, my world.

With my story finally finished, it was time for the big reveal. I could barely contain myself as I explained how funny my story was and how much Mrs Cook was going to laugh. I was convinced that my three sentences were as unique as they were spectacular. My masterpiece went something like this:

> **Mr Cook is in his car and Mrs Cook lives at the bottom of the hill and Mrs Cook has a car with Mr Cook and Mr Cook goes up the hill but it is icy so the car slides back down because it's icy!**

I know what you're thinking. Two words, eh? Booker. Prize.

Mrs Cook traced the words with her eyes while I watched her expectantly. When she reached the end, she threw her head back and lit up the sky with laughter. 'What a funny story! You are such a talented author!'

I believed her, 100%. And now you're reading my book, so I guess she was right!

A Christmas miracle

The best time in Mrs Cook's class was easily the preparation for Christmas – which, as all teachers of young children know, starts no later than the third week of September.

For what seemed like an eternity, our whole class screwed up little pieces of tissue paper and stuck them alongside bottle tops, dried pasta and bits of shiny paper to create beige camels, yellow straw for the manger and unpronounceable gifts for the baby Jesus – who for some unknown reason was always bright pink.

The finished collage covered an entire wall from floor to ceiling. Each evening, Mrs Cook would assemble the parts of the display we had made so far. In the morning, we ran into the classroom to admire and coo at the masterpiece we were creating. Our display included everything that Christmas stood for and more. If one of my classmates came in with a Spiderman sticker, Mrs Cook would find a space for that too.

As the Christmas holidays approached, there was only one piece of bare wall left – the spot reserved for our special star. While twenty-nine other children were busy covering themselves in glue, Mrs Cook called me over, placed her arm gently on my shoulder and whispered, 'Oh dear, we have a little problem on our hands and I need your help.' I was concerned but also intrigued. She was looking at the Christmas display – our classroom's central and most important element. What was wrong?

Mrs Cook increased the drama by instructing me not to panic so as not to worry the rest of the class. She told me that she was sure my 'superb' problem-solving skills would help her find a solution. I didn't know what superb meant but it sounded like an important word and made me feel braver. Her confidence more than made up for the lack of my own. Plus, her scheming tone both engaged and enrolled me. I had no idea what was required but I was already 100% in.

The daily investment Mrs Cook had paid into my emotional bank account had earned my trust and loyalty and I was ready to follow her to the ends of the earth.

She went on to explain, 'Oh, it's terrible. We've spent so much time working on this display and put in so much hard work, but I can't get the most important thing – the star – to stay up. I was here for hours last night. I've tried stapling it, I've tried sticky tape, I've tried glue. Nothing will make this star stay in place!'

The dilemma was compelling, and I wanted to help the human who had encouraged me so much. I took a deep breath and looked around the display and the room, searching for a spark of inspiration.

Nothing.

Mrs Cook filled the silence by pointing at the wall and saying things like, 'If only there were some way to fix the star to the wall. You know, something strong that could hold it. I don't know, like a nail …' Never slow to take a hint, I shifted my attention to the space where the wall met the ceiling. Here I suddenly spotted what must have been a three-inch nail poking out of the wall! Mrs Cook was right! I was going to solve this!

An idea slowly formed in my mind. Caught up in the excitement of what my discovery might mean, I summoned all the courage I had, pointed to the nail and ventured, 'Mrs Cook, what about that nail there?'

'Oh, that's very funny,' Mrs Cook replied, standing up and looking down at me with a smile. 'Thank you for trying to cheer me up.' She was pretending she thought I was doing the 'Not *that* nail, *this* nail, the one on my finger' joke, which the class loved so much. Did she not know I was trying to save the day? 'Right now, though, we really need a solution to this difficult star problem?'

Had I made a mistake? Was I wrong? No, there was definitely a nail there, and it did look strong enough to hold a mixed-media collaged star. But pressing the issue would mean contradicting a teacher – my favourite teacher. What to do?

I struggled to find the inner confidence needed to press my point home.

'I'm not doing the nail joke, honest, Mrs Cook. There really is a nail. Look, it's that massive one there!'

I pointed again, imploring her to look at the wall. She sighed and turned her head slowly towards the wall, only to pause for a moment, clutching a string of imaginary pearls around her neck and letting out a dramatic gasp that attracted the attention of the rest of the class.

'Ladies and gentlemen! Please stop what you're doing and look this way! This girl has only gone and saved Christmas!'

I grew three inches right there on the spot.

As I stood with her hand resting on my shoulder, facing my classmates, Mrs Cook went on to explain how I had single-handedly saved Christmas, leaving out the part where she stayed late the previous evening, stood on a chair and hammered a nail into the wall herself!

Not only was Mrs Cook's little Yuletide ruse such a massive boost to my confidence and self-esteem, an experience that has remained with me all these years later, but she also used it to illustrate that if you see something that could solve a problem, you should always speak up. More than once if necessary. As she was fond of saying: 'Champions never give up!'

To hammer (see what I did there?) the point home, as the bell rang for break time, this previously nervous six-year-old stood at the front of the class, next to the best teacher in the world, arms in the air and swaying from side to side, leading twenty-nine residually sticky children in a chorus of 'We Are the Champions' by Queen. Every time I hear that song today, it makes me cry with gratitude for the woman who knew that for me to become a champion, first, I had to believe it was possible. And then creatively applied her Oscar-winning acting ability, unconditional positive regard and plain and simple love to make it so.

The sanctuary of school toilets

'So, they get a ginormous sucker, right, and they put it on your face, yeah, and they yank it back and they suck your eye out, then they look at it from all angles, then they put it in their mouth and suck all the dirt off, and then they shove it back in the socket.'

We'll come to the sex ed lesson later but, in the meantime, the above description of how an impending eye test would be carried out was definitely the most terrifying thing I'd heard at school.

It was described to me by a classmate, possibly hell-bent on revenge after an unfortunate incident involving half a packet of Spangles that resulted in her being fired from Brownies. Her description was all the information I needed for the thin layer of protection I had built around myself to be breached. My fear rose, I panicked and, in response to a teaching assistant simply inviting me to finish the activity I was doing in time for break, I threw my chair to the ground, ran out of the classroom and locked myself in the abiding sanctuary known to all us traumatised kids – the toilet cubicle.

Once there, time stalled. Even though the doors were low enough for a decent-sized adult to peer over, I felt safe. I banked on locking the door and ramming my feet up against it being enough to render the cubicle safe – or at least ginormous sucker-proof! If anyone did come in, I'd see them first and scream blue murder! I waited in terror and held my breath when I heard my name called out a couple of times. As time passed, I didn't know how to go back. It slowly dawned on me that my plan to stay in the cubicle forever had several flaws, but I was too afraid to deviate from it.

During the peace of assembly, Mrs Cook came into the toilets and sat in the cubical next to the only one that was closed. With the general lack of self-regulation in our class, I'm sure she probably fancied locking the door, claiming 'sanctuary' and having a little cry herself. Instead, she spoke gently to me, explaining that everyone gets scared, just like everyone gets hungry or tired. She reminded me of how brave I was and listed triumphs from my learning journey – my story of the car on the hill, Christmas Stargate. I sat listening to her telling me that she was proud of me, and painting a picture of me as a strong, capable and clever little girl. She took the time to listen to my counterargument before reasserting what she believed to be true. It was as if she saw me at that moment as a tangled ball of string and set about painstakingly unravelling me, smoothing me out and winding me back up neatly before asking for anything from me.

Only once some form of equilibrium had been re-established did she broach the subject of the eye test, listen to me rambling on about suckers and Spangles and eyes being yanked out in between snotty sobs, and invite me out of the cubicle.

I must have looked a sorry state when I finally opened the toilet door. She stood looking at me, her head tilted slightly to one side, and then she smiled that same smile of genuine delight and opened her arms. I ran to her and hugged her as if she was my grandad's leg. Enveloped in one of her furry brown sweaters I was overwhelmed with relief and gratitude. Her light created a way out of the darkness for me and it didn't require the effort of wrapping words around the dripping wet splodge of a picture in my head.

Goodbye grandad

One day, when the sun was shining strong outside, my grandad died. In the midst of the topsy-turvy world of grieving and uncertainty, there was a funeral I wasn't allowed to attend and a wedding I didn't want to.

As she watched her husband of thirty years deteriorate, my nan had begun to laugh less and cry more. I silently noted the worry wrinkle on her face as she sat by his bed in the living room and tried to get him to drink sips of water. Less tolerant of me and my (now four years old and slightly more fun but still annoying) little brother, she instructed us to be 'seen and not heard' and no longer had time for connection in the form of the weekly wrestling match with my unruly Afro and grandad's glossy hair slop. The loss of her husband's income alongside the pressure of working two cleaning jobs and caring for two children and a sick husband alone ate away at her. Less than a week after his death, my biological mother returned home with an announcement. She had a new boyfriend and was pregnant with child number three.

My grandad's death had kickstarted what was going to be a long winter. The new boyfriend found himself on the receiving end of several side-eye looks from my nan, but none of the sass she was known for. Losing her sweetheart and best friend dampened her enthusiasm for life and my nan retreated into standby mode, going from steadfast captain of the ship to reluctant and exhausted passenger.

On a regular Friday, I skipped away from Mrs Cook's class unaware that I would never return. Another adult I loved that I didn't get to say goodbye to. The next day, a defeated version of my nan took me and Paul shopping, bought us each a new outfit to wear and dropped us off outside a building with lots of steps in an unfamiliar and scary part of town we'd never been to before.

I didn't blame my grief-stricken nan when she left me in charge of an unhappy four-year-old who was missing Saturday morning TV at what turned out to be the registry office where our biological mother was marrying our new stepfather and soon-to-be abuser. Or for failing to rescue us after the wedding when we were taken to live in Uncle Mick's 'bed and breakfast' or, in my nan's words, 'bed and breakfast my arse – a bleddy bed and brothel is what it is!'

Our new life was a baptism of sh*t. The first night, our new stepfather barked instructions at a shell-shocked and terrified Paul and me to sit in a corner with a blanket over our heads while he and my biological mother had sex in the only bed in the room. The following days didn't improve. Our new routine consisted of Paul and I being left alone while my biological mother and stepfather spent their honeymoon out partying.

Banished from the room in the day (Uncle Mick said it was his 'office'), Paul and I spent several long days and nights unsupervised, hungry and still wearing our wedding outfits, without pyjamas or a change of clothes. Sat on the doorstep outside Uncle Mick's house I noted a stream of snappily dressed men park on the drive, walk past us, stay for a while and then leave. I'd never seen anyone dressed in a suit and tie (and went on to learn that such attire is usually reserved for court cases or church christenings) so I figured these guys must be millionaires. Driven by hunger I established a lucrative side hustle scamming Uncle Mick's friends out of 50p a time by promising to keep an eye on their Ford Cortinas while they were inside. Of course, as soon as they were at the reception desk we legged it to the chip shop, leaving their Batmobiles at the mercy of anyone brave enough to have a go at grand theft auto in the under-resourced area we lived in.

Some days it worked, some days it didn't. Some days we ate, some days we didn't. After a while, Uncle Mick got fed up with the (literal) 'cheeky little beggars' sat on his doorstep all day long and gave my parents their marching orders.

I kind of understood why my nan refused to get out of the car on her weekly visits to our new house – a condemned three-storey terrace. With the top floor made uninhabitable by broken windows and floorboards and the wind from the basement cellar rushing up the chimney and out of the fireplaces, it was a long way from her world of Calor gas heaters and acres of hand-knitted blankets. We were squatting in our own filth and, thanks to the last residents who had kicked the box of the electric meter, using the same 50p again and again to make the lights work.

My nan parked outside and passed neatly folded piles of freshly washed and ironed clothes and belongings out of the rolled-down window of her Triumph Dolomite. Walking to our front door I took long, deep and enthusiastic inhalations of those piles of laundry, languishing in the scent of Fairy fabric conditioner. We never got to wear the clean clothes, play with our beloved toys, or read our well-thumbed story books. Out of place in our threadbare house, they were bagged up as soon as my nan's car drove away. Anything of value that made its way into our house (or ended up there by 'falling off the back of a lorry') was quickly sold by our stepfather for, as he repeatedly told Paul and I while rubbing his hands with delight, 'mi beer money'.

Confused, unsettled and weakened by hunger and the lack of security in our new life, the dynamic between my little brother and myself changed. At the beginning, we both cried – a lot. However, with no responsible adult available, Paul looked to me to take care of him. Luckily, even though Mrs Cook was miles away in another part of the city and I no longer had any contact with her, she had made bravery an accessible trait. As the eldest, I took it upon myself to pass on the gift and teach Paul how to embrace it. Predictably, my four-year-old charge wasn't a natural knight at that early stage in his life and, seeing as I was already so experienced at bossing him around, I quickly took on the role of parent. The upside of this is that it allowed me to disassociate from the horror of our new home by focusing on being in charge and keeping us both safe. I retreated into a state of human-doing rather than human-being.

I tried to create pictures in my mind that made sense of our harrowing existence since the death of my grandad. With no sense to be made, my young brain looked for someone to blame. I didn't blame my nan for any of it, or my biological mother, or even my new stepfather, and it certainly wasn't Paul's fault either. I blamed myself. I reasoned that I must have done something wrong to deserve the devastating lifestyle shift. Something so bad, it triggered a downward step on the social mobility ladder from a poor-but-loved working-class kid to an at best ignored and at worst despised feral six-year-old in a 'criminal class' family with sole responsibility for keeping her little brother alive and quiet enough not to annoy the adults that other people referred to as our parents.

Just as my hope that life would return to what it was faded, I was thrown a lifeline. Something so monumental it not only rekindled my dwindling hope, it gave me something to look forward to, relax in and live for.

School.

Categorising adults

I never got to tell her before I left, but Mrs Cook was a bona fide Category 1 adult.

After we'd left the bed and brothel, we upgraded to a condemned terrace house round the corner. My parents were too preoccupied to enrol us in school, so Paul and I occupied ourselves by spending as much time as we could outside. Despite the obvious dangers of two young children roaming the streets where drug dealers, gang leaders and sexual predators felt emboldened enough not to hide, it was still safer than inside the unsafe house that was now our home.

I turned seven without anyone noticing and, deciding that it marked my transition to being a 'grown-up girl', I began to devise a system for keeping myself and my brother safe. It was all about defining how much we could trust the adults around us. Some adults seemed nice, but then so had my stepfather at the beginning. I began to systematically categorise every adult we met and instructed Paul, who I considered to be far too kind-hearted and trusting, to keep his eyes on me so I could flash the correct number of fingers indicating their score. This secret code was a way of knowing who could be trusted, and who definitely couldn't.

A Category 1 adult loves you unconditionally. I mean they *really* love you. Category 1 adults show delight at the thought of spending time with you. Their faces and body language leak the joy of genuine connection while hanging out and chatting with you. They're not looking at the clock or distracted by their phones. They're interested and it's tangible. You can see it, hear it, feel it. Mrs Cook was definitely a Category 1 adult.

Most of the other adults I met were firmly Category 2s. Category 2 adults don't *love* you but they do *like* you. You don't have to be scared of a Category 2 because they are not going to physically hurt you, which was an enormous relief for me. However, on the flip side, you're basically a bit of a burden. For example, the Category 2s in school have a tonne of stuff to do. Meetings to attend, books to mark, detentions to supervise, etc. They are happy to chat but as displays don't put themselves up, there is a hint of a hurried air about their interactions. My defining factor for Category 2s was those adults who were with you because they were paid to be. So yeah, they'll never give you a black eye, but you are just that little bit in the way.

Harsh, isn't it? Harsh, but necessary for two kids to protect themselves. Worse still, my categorisation didn't mirror the world of UK football. Once categorised, adults rarely moved up a league. I had to make a snap decision about whether you were a safe adult or not and I couldn't afford to get it wrong. I'm sure I misclassified a fair few Category 1s as Category 2s because they were trying to do their best in a system that allowed little time to breathe and take stock. Anyone preoccupied with, 'Right, come on, get this, move, move, move, quick, quick, quick' wouldn't have the time to sit and wait long enough for me to try and find the words to describe what was happening to me at home.[6]

---

6 'What about the Category 3s?' I hear you cry! Now we're talking. A Category 3 adult is either dangerous or an idiot or a dangerous idiot and are to be avoided at all costs.

My powers of categorisation were not foolproof – something I discovered to my cost. The only adults I could talk to about what was going on at home were Category 1s but I made the mistake of disclosing to three Category 2s before I was believed.

Mrs Cook, however, was a totally bona fide Category 1 WAGOLL.[7]

Sex education

The next four years were spent in and out of foster care but to see how much impact Mrs Cook had in my life, we have to fast forward six years to an eleven-year-old me sat in a Year 7 sex ed class.

Our PE teacher drew what I'm assuming was the shortest straw in the staffroom lottery and 'won' the prize of delivering the sex ed/period talk. To paint a picture for those lucky enough to avoid doing PE in the UK high school education system circa 1982, think maroon tracksuit, Gola trainers and a vertical zip pocket on her right chest where she kept her Benson and Hedges.

Mrs G was actually a fantastic PE teacher but had a slight tendency to give short shrift to anyone who was not match fit. I had quick reflexes, was a fast runner and loved hitting balls with sticks so I quickly found a natural home in all things sport-flavoured. I loved the focus and challenge of shooting hoops, hurling discs or jumping (either over poles or into long, thin sandpits) and I quickly became a rising star who would go on to represent the school in numerous sporting fixtures. The skills I learned through sport include the experience of being part of a team/family, persistence, commitment, discipline and self-leadership – but most of all PE taught me what it was to belong.[8] Mrs G was a brilliant coach, only she lost a few points for offering to forge get-out-of-PE-free notes for the kids with asthma.

Determined to build our characters, she used to make us do cross-country, around a council estate where there was no country to cross. The combination

---

7   What A Good One Looks Like – and I don't mean an exemplary exam answer – YOU are a living WAGOLL!

8   It baffles and frustrates me that PE is often seen as the poor relation, when it should be the centre of the curriculum. After safeguarding, what's more important than your physical and mental health? Not to mention the myriad of life skills!

of being outside and running was liberating for me. However, the part I deeply despised was the PE kit. For some bizarre reason, and probably one made at a meeting in an office block far removed from a school playing field with zero women in attendance, my PE kit consisted of a pleated-within-an-inch-of-its-life micro skirt (reserved for the high holy days) and regular day-to-day attire of navy blue hip-hugging PE knickers that reached all the way up to your chest. Even if you managed to stretch your non-stretchy Artex t-shirt down, you were still running around the streets in what was essentially a pair of undercrackers.

Obviously, Mrs G would accompany us, but rather than run, she found it more prudent to tag along in her car. Driving alongside us, she would occasionally wind down the passenger window of her clapped-out Granada to let the built-up fog of cigarette smoke escape and share some encouragement. 'Get a bloody move on girls. It's nearly break!'[9]

Back to sex ed.

Here we are, a class of eleven-year-olds reluctantly sat in the gym when we could be outside in our hockey studs tearing up and down the pitch. Mrs G is unsuccessfully battling the echoes of heckling and general malcontent as she tries to explain we're going to bleed every month for the next fifty years of our life – and will be wearing PE knickers while running around the streets twice a week for the next five, regardless. Are you getting a picture of how well this lesson went down? After unsuccessfully trying to get us on side, Mrs G does the only thing left to do – she sticks a video on.

I'm sitting at the back with my mates.

And we're laughing.

And we're watching.

And I'm watching.

And my throat is getting tight.

And I am coughing to try to clear my throat.

But it's not working.

And my chest gets tight and I feel like I can't breathe.

I panic and frantically look around to see if anyone else is having a heart attack.

Nope, it's just me.

---

9 That was safeguarding in the 1980s. Thankfully it's moved on a bit since then.

I glance back at the screen.

The seeds. The tubes. The eggs.

And then it happens. In a flood of dam-bursting technicolour horror, I realise that what my stepfather has been forcing me to do for the last five years since I was six is how women get pregnant.

And I die.

In that moment, I became a thief. I stole the guilt and shame belonging to my perpetrator and made it mine.

I die – but only on the inside.

I say 'inside' because in my short time at high school, I'd already learned to keep my guard well and truly up. I had perfected 'the look'. You know the one. ASD – angry, scowling and defiant. It's meant to keep you (the adult I don't yet trust) away from me. Only in this situation, I am at the back of the gym surrounded by students and with no way out.

What would your next course of action be in that situation?

Strap yourself in for the part of this story that no amount of healing has soothed. As I sat in shock, no longer hearing the shrieks of laughter coming from my friends on either side of me and trying to work out what to do next, a thought dawned on me. Like a ship in a storm, that thought charted a course directly to my belief system and anchored itself, causing me to act.

There is no point telling anyone. The adults in school all know what's happening to me at home, and they are okay with it.

Some of my teachers looked at me in the same way my parents did, with the same annoyed look on their faces. Some *said* the same words and used the same exact phrases as my parents, which made my ears prick up and my defence systems jump to high alert: 'You've let yourself down and you've let us down' and 'Just be a good girl'. Some adults in school actually *did* the same thing to me – at home, I was locked in a cellar as punishment. At school, I'm detained in isolation. A much nicer room but it still said the same thing to me. 'You're not good enough. We don't want you here. You don't belong.' I draw the conclusion that the adults at school, my teachers, obviously all agreed with my parents. Worse still I feared what they all thought was true.

I am cheap. I am dirty. I am worthless. I am guilty. I am wrong.

So, I run.

My only goal is to get out of the gym and away from any other human. I need a quiet place to explode. Somewhere enclosed. A sanctuary.

A toilet cubical.

The toilets in the gym changing rooms reek of disinfectant so powerful it feels like it could dissolve the blazer off of your back.

The smell overcomes me, and I run into the first cubicle and desperately clutch the broken black toilet seat as I vomit into the bowl.

If we were sat together now I'd encourage you to pause and breathe. If this feels heartbreaking, it's because it was. And here's another truth, because of my Everyday Heroes, heartbreak wasn't the last word.

Slumped on the floor I realise I'm crying, which heaps additional shame onto the pile I'm already digesting. I grab a handful of green scratchy paper towels. Not to wipe my tears but to clean up the bile from the floor – because you can't leave a mess in the toilets, right?

Then I run. There's nothing else to do. I run.

Away from school.

Away from my family, from Paul and the latest two brothers, a baby and a toddler who also relied on me for protection, food, nurture and love.

I give up. I stop believing in hope. And I run.

There is no way Mrs Cook would wear this

Accustomed as I was to wandering around the streets on weekends with my siblings, it was a different story alone, hypervigilant and dressed in a school uniform. I knew well enough to stay away from the main streets where Uncle Mick's bed and brothel was based. For the first couple of nights, I slept in a den some kids had built in a derelict house. By day three I was a wreck.

Being cold, tired, hungry and scared was still better than the alternative of going home. I was one of the lucky ones though. I was rescued. Many young people with my background never find safety away from the streets. This is where their hope ends. On the third night, I met an incredible human being called Jason.

Jason reminded me of my other five Everyday Heroes. He saw me, he listened to me, he showed me compassion and he *saw* me. An expert in with-ness, he met me where I was and stood next to me in the chaotic fire that was my life. When we first met, he took me to a pub. He bought me a much-needed meal. He even found me somewhere to stay. And that's how I came to be standing in a changing room a few days later, holding a dress.

Jason had taken me shopping for some new clothes. I was so excited to try on the outfit that it wasn't until I was standing in the changing room looking at it on the hanger that I realised it wasn't a dress that was appropriate for an eleven-year-old girl to wear. And Jason wasn't a kind benefactor – he was a predator.

If there's one thing that gang leaders and dealers excel at, it's the ability to make you feel like you belong.

I've often thought schools could learn a lot from pimps in that department.

Something I continue to unpack today is how quickly kindness can mutate into danger. At school I could never understand how adults could so easily assume that I would trust and buy into what they were saying just because they were adults. Thankfully, nowadays, I'm surrounded by incredible friends and a husband that has done more to keep me grounded over the last twenty-five years than any human on this planet. Trust is hard-earned. I've struggled with that my whole life and I'm still learning that my first instinct is not always the right one.

So ...

I'm standing in a changing room.

I'm holding an inappropriate outfit for an eleven-year-old.

I don't know the phrase 'sexual exploitation', but I know instinctively that I'm not safe.

I'm all alone in the world, apart from Jason lurking outside the changing room ...

Freezeframe there and let me ask you something. How much difference do you think you could make to that little girl at that precise moment? On a scale of one to ten if one is nothing and ten is everything, what's your number? Remember, you're not even in the room. You don't know where she is. But in that moment, what score do you get? What story do you tell about your own impact?

If it's anything less than eleven hundred, you're sorely mistaken.

I know that for a fact because I was that little girl, standing in that changing room, holding that 'dress'. And as I stood there, one crystal clear thought came into my mind:

There is no way that Mrs Cook would wear this outfit!

Out of nowhere. I haven't set eyes on her in years, but it doesn't matter. Suddenly, I'm brave. I drop the outfit. I walk out of the changing room, out of the shop, across a four-lane main road, and straight into the police station.

Once inside, I do what I think adults do in police stations: I slam my hands on the counter and declare loudly, 'I demand the right to remain silent!'

That's the power of legacy. The hallmark of an Everyday Hero is what happens when they're no longer in the room. I wish I could tell you that this was a complete turning point to a happily ever after ending. It wasn't a moment in which I became fearless, wrapping my past pain up in a Tiffany gift box and skipping away to happiness. It was, however, a tiny crack of bravery in the turreted fortress of fear I lived in that went on to lay the ground for future strides. Working out what safety looks like in relationships continued to be a lifetime quest for me. I've learned that what I missed out on through a lack of being parented as a child takes an exponentially longer time to grasp as an adult trying to parent your inner child.

Back to the police station ...

At first, and still without the words to describe what had happened, I played hardball and refused to give my name or address, naively figuring they would find me new parents and I could go back home later and kidnap my siblings. I don't know if you have ever found yourself on the receiving end of being questioned by the police, but these guys were not to be trifled with and wore me down in about ten minutes with their offer of a bottle of Panda Cola and a packet of pickled onion Monster Munch. Though I still wasn't able to give them any actual details they could see I was in distress and incredibly upset from my experience. I refused point blank to go home, swearing I'd run away again. I must have been convincing because the guy at the desk (and the keeper of the Monster Munch) asked me where I would go if I could choose.

That was easy. To my nan's house.

I found bravery because of Mrs Cook, because of the impact of Mrs Cook. This is what I'm talking about. She saved my life and she wasn't even there. The true mark of a great teacher, leader or influencer? It's what happens when you're no longer in the room.

Years later, I stand once again in the same playground where I used to run free and face Mrs Cook. I failed to find the words to express the wide-arching gratitude welling up in my heart. My first Everyday Hero kept her hand on my arm.

Mrs Cook: I am *so* proud of you.

Then the smile. That smile.

After she had affirmed how she felt about me, Mrs Cook turned away, crouching down to comfort a small boy whose face was a mess of tears and snot. She didn't seem to remember me specifically – I was just one of hundreds of children whose lives she'd touched. But watching her work her magic in that moment transported me back to the safety of the familiar psychedelic cocoon of her class. There she was, doing exactly what she'd always done, what she'd done for me all those years ago. Looking past the tears and mess to see the heart and humanity. Looking behind the front.

I watched in awe as she spoke calmly and gently to the boy and every other child who came up to her with some emergency or other. That was Mrs Cook. She wasn't looking for a medal or an award, she didn't need to take a photo or get me to sign a form and send it to Ofsted as proof of progress. She'd seen me, heard me and checked that I was doing well. She was pleased that I'd gone on to fulfil my potential, and she then got back to making sure her next class did too.

Every time I stand on stage and speak to educators, I think of Mrs Cook. She had no idea that her consistent kindness and unshakeable belief would one day save me from a predator or that the little girl in the brown jumper collecting toilet rolls would actually become that fantastic teacher she predicted.

Mrs Cook simply tied a golden rope of possibility around my waist when I was six years old and anchored the other end firmly in my future. Even in my darkest moments – and there were some pretty midnight black ones – that rope remained. She broke bravery down into bite-sized chunks. Today, when I speak on stages around the world, I'm not just sharing my story – I'm living proof of Mrs Cook's legacy.

That's what makes Mrs Cook an Everyday Hero. She was driven to do what she did because it was the right thing to do and it fulfilled her. Not because there were boxes to tick or targets to hit. She was clear, probably from early on in her career, on what success looked like for her and, in this way, she has managed to future-proof herself as a teacher and stay in an incredibly demanding profession, changing lives every single year, one smile at a time. Mrs Cook chose curiosity rather than fear.

I walked away knowing that just as she'd been my Everyday Hero decades ago, she was still quietly working her magic. Different children, same impact. As the first of my five Everyday Heroes, Mrs Cook didn't just transform my life – she showed me how to live it bravely.

Mrs Cook's Legacy

Writing this chapter has been an emotional rollercoaster for me! Just like when I deliver keynotes on stage, I'm speaking from a place of healed wounds, not open scars. However, that doesn't negate the immense sadness I experience remembering the constant despair I felt as a child. At the same time, that sadness is dwarfed by the knowledge of Everyday Heroes in classrooms all over the world today.

One mistake I still beat myself up for making as a teacher myself is the 'Write about what you did at the weekend/in the holidays' exercise. I struggle to forgive myself because I remember the impossible situation that put me in as a child. I knew that lying was wrong but if I had written the truth about what was happening at home with the obligatory accompanying picture, I was terrified that my teachers would faint, get cross or accuse me of lying. Either way I was sure I'd be guaranteed to be in trouble – at school and at home. Even though I hated myself for lying more than I hated myself for causing the beatings I deserved, I would sit miserably writing something I'd made up or seen on TV. I became the Mistress of Masking.

If you work directly with children, you might recognise some of what I've described – the child who flinches at loud noises, who arrives hungry, who struggles to belong. This is classic trigger-and-response stuff. When people (especially children) behave in a way we consider to be unacceptable we tend to start with the 'What?' of a situation, whereas the answer and solution tend to be rooted in the 'Why?' Mrs Cook didn't have today's safeguarding training or trauma-informed practice guidelines. What she did have was an unshakeable belief in the power of human connection and the courage to keep showing up with compassion.

What I learned very early on was that the way school was set up – the expectations and assumptions about students turning up ready to learn – made it difficult for me to belong. I was a chaos navigator, and the education system seemed to be set up for order navigators, those who turned up ready to learn.

When it all became too much, I did object. I wanted to let my teachers know that I could no longer hold it all in, but this was a form of communication they labelled as 'challenging behaviour'. I'd have aced any test that involved burying the desire to scream but no child ever received house points for that.

Mrs Cook, however, had a tendency to meet people where they were. She saw it as her job to find me and take me with her. Not to wait for me to catch up with her.

Everything I knew about myself, other than what I picked up from the few (stable) adults I'd had in my short life, came from what Mrs Cook told me about me. If she had said I was impossible to teach, then I would have believed her. Those three words would have become my bedrock foundation. Impossible. To. Teach. Who I was, who I became, what I went on to do or not do, how I behaved or didn't – everything would have been built on top of those three words.

Of course, this isn't a fairytale and I didn't give her an easy ride, Category 1 or not. Like every adult I met, I scanned her for signs of deceit. Could I really trust her, right here, right now? Mrs Cook, though, had the whole package. Positive and reinforcing words, a neutral tone and non-threatening body language – all delivered consistently, regardless of what state I was in.

Mrs Cook's legacy still shows up in my life today. I talk about being 10% braver, a gem I magpied from the fabulous Sue Cowley at a WomenEd[10] conference. 10% is a great first step. You don't have to start an actual revolution. For you, being 10% braver might be simply raising your hand in a meeting. Or deciding your past will no longer be a script for your future. Or leaving that toxic

---

10 See https://www.womened.com/.

relationship you know is hurting you. You are just that bit braver, developing your courage in small, incremental steps by saying yes in a place where you always said 'No way, I can't do that' before and then building on it. The result? You stop letting fear 'drive your bus', and you open the door to becoming your 'full-fat self'. A semi-skimmed life is for milk, not for humans.

The antidote? Be a human WAGOLL.[11] Be the adult a child looks at and thinks, 'I'd like to be like them. It looks kinda fun.'

Be Mrs Cook: Reflections

1. **Be 10% braver**

    What could your life look like if you were just 10% braver today? Not under-crackers-over-your-tights-superhero-type brave, just a small step outside of your comfort zone. Make that step as small as possible. Got one? Good. Now take it. Remember, bravery isn't feeling fearless – it's feeling the fear and choosing to move forward anyway.

2. **Celebrate your wins**

    We're brilliant at celebrating others but rubbish at acknowledging our own triumphs. Swap that never-ending to-do list for a to-be list![12] What have you already accomplished that deserves celebration? Remember, Usain Bolt takes less than ten seconds to run 100 meters but then spends a good five minutes on a victory lap! It's time to wave your knickers in the air like you just don't care.

3. **Reframe your challenge**

    Mrs Cook didn't see a terrified child, she saw the potential for making bravery a habit. Consider one of the bigger challenges you're facing right now. How could you reframe that into an opportunity to uncover strength you didn't know you had? You're basically adding gold paint to your palette.

---

11 What A Good One Looks Like.
12 Here's a sobering thought ... you're going to die with an unfinished to do list (#justsaying) so be more human being and less human doing.

4. **Be a human WAGOLL**

   What A Good One Looks Like isn't just a teaching device. You're a walking, talking example of possibility for every child you encounter. Whether you're in a classroom, a parent or simply shopping for this week's supply of chocolate Hobnobs, mini humans are watching! What version of adulthood are you modelling today?

5. **Shield yourself**

   There's no way Mrs Cook spent fifteen years as a teacher without a kick-ass wellbeing strategy! Invest in a Vibranium-strength shield[13] to help with your own wellbeing. Create your own SHIELD acronym for the six things that protect and sustain you. Mine includes **S**unshine, **H**ealth, **I**ntegrity, **E**veryday Heroes, **L**aughter and **D**reaming Bigger. What are your six go-tos for when life tries to knock you over?

6. **Find your Everyday Heroes**

   Who are the Mrs Cooks in your life? The ones who saw something in you that you couldn't yet see in yourself? Send them a message today thanking them for their impact. If they're no longer with us, pay their gift forward to someone who needs it.

7. **Say goodbye to should stories**

   Mrs Cook added bright yellow to my grey palette. What limiting beliefs are keeping your life monochrome? Stick a colourful hat on, stand in front of the mirror and talk yourself up for 15 seconds. Take those negative statements (you know, the things you keep saying to yourself about not being good enough) and rewrite them into something more accurate. Your past is not a script for your future.

8. **Check yourself before you wreck yourself**

   On a scale of 'I'm fine, said through gritted teeth' to 'tiptoeing through tulips without a care in the world', how close are you to burnout? Use my personal roadmap to future-proof yourself.

   - Suffering (in pain and staying there)
   - Surviving (a pretty low bar, I mean, you can survive on a ventilator)
   - Thriving (overcoming obstacles and refusing to let your past become a script for your future)

---

13 Wakanda Forever!

- Driving change (helping others to interpret their own limiting narratives)
- Truly alive (full-fat freedom baby!)

Living outside your integrity is exhausting. Next time you're about to make a decision, ask yourself: 'Is this aligned with my values?'

9. **Create belonging**

    Create the space Mrs Cook created for me. Belonging isn't earned through compliance – it's offered through connection. Think about a student, friend or colleague who may feel like they are not enough. What small act can you do today to help them see themselves and their value?

10. **Build your values lighthouse**

    Lighthouses are great to visit on a sunny day but they come into their own when the sky is black, the waves are high and the storm is raging. Mrs Cook shone a beam so bright it steered me away from the rocks years later as I stood in a changing room holding a dress. You can't shine a light if your own foundations are shaky. Spend some time pinpointing your top three key values. If you get stuck, ask a friend what you radiate.

Mr Williams
The One Who Taught Me Truth

I'd spent a fair amount of the eight years I'd been on the planet being ill, but I could not remember experiencing anything like this. My head throbbed and I was throwing up so much that I couldn't get to the end of my bed, let alone school – even for Mr William's fantastical classes. A visit to the doctor was rare as it meant giving outsiders a window into our world so, instead, my stepfather put a sick bucket next to the mattress on the floor that was my bed. I used it so much it was half-full and stank, but he didn't come back to empty it. The flip side of that was that he stayed away from my room at night as well.

With me out of action, there was no one to take my brother to school, which meant he spent the week at home too. Even though Paul had seen me do it every day, he struggled to run the military operation required to get a baby and a toddler up, dressed and fed in the morning. I simultaneously loved him as a brother whilst hating him for being only six and useless without my help. After hearing him crying in distress downstairs, even though I still felt dizzy and faint, I had no choice but to get up and resume my caregiving duties.

In the front room, the TV blared loudly as usual. My biological mother sat on the sofa surrounded by ashtrays and half-drunk abandoned mugs of tea from previous days. Her friend sat next to her. Every time I'd seen the friend, she was either spaced out or had already left the planet entirely. They both sat staring at the TV, smoking, drinking and oblivious to the crying baby and toddler my six-year-old brother was struggling to pacify.

My biological mother didn't seem to notice me arrive, or that I was quite ill, and instructed me to bring a less full ashtray over to her. I was slower than usual and the friend, seeing how sick I was, advised my biological mother that I should be given bread soaked in milk to settle my stomach. Finding a few slices of slightly mouldy Mother's Pride in the kitchen, she cut off the crusts and soaked them in a saucer of milk – milk that had been left out of the fridge and was past its best. The saucer was placed on the floor for me to eat.

Even in my headache haze, I knew this lady had confused caring for a sick child with the advice that *Blue Peter* had mistakenly given for feeding hedgehogs.[1] I

---

1   Hedgehogs are lactose intolerant so please don't feed them this.

refused. My capacity for putting up with crap from adults was massively reduced by the throbbing in my head, the churning in my stomach and the thought of kneeling on the filthy floor to eat wet bread. In a flash, my biological mother lurched towards me, her cigarette bobbing from the side of her mouth as she spat out a familiar tirade of insults, 'You ungrateful little ...' I felt her nails press into my skin as she grabbed the scruff of my neck and pressed me downward towards the floor, forcing my face into the mixture.

Sour milk slime seeped into my nostrils. Face down and too weak to struggle I could hear the sound of both women laughing. Somewhere in the house a baby was crying. Paul. Where was he? If he saw this he'd be even more scared and I didn't have the strength to reassure him.

Fighting the urge to pass out I turned my head to see the sight that extinguished the last bit of hope and fight I had left in me: my baby brother trying to keep hold of a screaming and wriggling toddler and looking at me in pure horror with silent tears streaming down his cheeks.

The Weirdo from Wales

In my expert opinion, Mr Williams was a liar.

An enthusiastically sweaty and definitely weird Welsh liar.

Within the first few seconds of meeting him, and before the fateful day with the cricket bat, I had Mr Williams down as a Category 3 adult. Not dangerous at all but, on a scale of one to ten, he was off the shizang. He had the energy of a caffeinated squirrel, a booming voice and wore jackets that didn't quite fit with sleeves that were two to three business days away from his actual wrists.

But like so many things I believed, I was totally wrong about him.

About the same height as the tallest eleven-year-olds in our school, Mr Williams had a wiry ball of mostly-brown-but-with-grey-tips hair. Not an Afro but certainly Afro-adjacent. He'd presumably grown it out in an attempt to add a few inches of height. His eyes were mostly covered by an untamable fringe that he constantly tried to control by blowing upwards out of the corner of his mouth. And, because having a barnet that meant you had to go through doors sideways wasn't enough hair, he finished off the look with a moustache and beard combo so huge it required its own passport.

He always wore a jacket, shirt and tie, which made him stand out from the other teachers, who favoured the un-ironed-chic look, and his booming voice and energetic style of teaching meant he would end up with extremely noticeable sweat marks at the armpits. On top of all that, his jacket was too tight and his trousers were too short. I tried to help by giving him the fashion advice I'd heard my nan dish out to people: 'Hey, sir, you should put some jam on your shoes and invite your trousers down for tea!'

Depending on how bad things were at home, I arrived at school as a reluctant Jekyll and Hyde character. I silently hated the abusive adults at home, but somehow only allowed the fume to seep out at school against the nurturing adults. I felt guilty all the time for that, but I felt like my school adults were lulling me into a false and temporary sense of security during the day. No matter how positive they were, I still had to return back to hell at 3.15pm every day.

My inability to self-regulate, and the rollercoaster up-and-down behaviour traits this caused, landed me in a special class. An environment designed for children who benefit from a little extra input. It was basically a nurture group before nurture groups were called nurture groups. The Annexe Class was full of kids who were experienced chaos navigators. Days were one long riot with a bit of teaching thrown in if there was ever a lull and a teacher who we hadn't already exhausted.

Our classroom was on a ground-floor annexe just off the dining hall. This arrangement meant that the noise we made didn't disturb anyone and we had space to run around when the need arose, as it often did. An added bonus, it also meant that we were always first in the dinner queue. It was here that the eight-year-old firecracker I was met Mr Williams, a phenomenal human male who lived under the misapprehension that he had any chance of being in charge of the class. We clashed immediately. What's more, he was an easy target as there was so much about his appearance that invited constructive criticism. In contrast to Mrs Cook being a 1970s style queen, Mr Williams' stylist clearly secretly hated him. His outfits and general way of being earned him the nickname the Weirdo from Wales.

I don't remember much about the academic work we did, apart from the fact that I had not yet received my Times Table Certificate from the head so had to endure extra maths, which Mr Williams tried to make more exciting by turning multiplication into dragon-counting games. I preferred to sit for hours sorting the huge box of mismatched Scottish Maths Project cards into colours and number order rather than completing any of the activities on them. However, when it came to anything to do with storytelling or drama, I shone.

The knight who rescued the princess

Mr Williams had two passions: teaching and being Welsh. Everything we learned was related back to Wales, in some way connected to Welsh values or had been invented in Wales. Also, he was always banging on about dragons and had a bright red Welsh one on his pencil tin and mug.

He was excited about our learning and quick to praise us when we persevered. He was the first adult to tell me that I had a 'vivid imagination' and that, if I used it, I could 'do something great in the world'. It connected with Mrs Cook's pipedream of becoming a teacher. He often encouraged us to make up and act out our own stories based on one stimulus or another (either dragons, knights or dragons *with* knights) and then got us to write them down as plays or narratives.

All of the scripts and stories I wrote were finished with the only ending I could imagine happening – everyone dying at the end. Mr Williams was a firm believer in the whole teacher as Devil's advocate thing and asked me what would happen if all the characters lived instead. He often told us no question was stupid, so even though this one clearly was, I thought about it, and replied with something I thought was reserved for 'proper' stories in books. 'Living happily ever after?' He raised his substantial eyebrows in a way that said 'You're onto something there. What would that be like?' Not demanding, not correcting – inviting me to imagine a different possibility. His questions weren't about changing my stories, they were about showing me I had the power to write new endings.

And there it was again, that disconnect. My home life told me that I was unlikely to live past primary school. That seems horrific to write but the true horror was that I remembered having accepted it as fact. The world was an unsafe place and kids like me just didn't get their happily ever afters. Mr Williams' question opened up the possibility of a different reality – what could be possible if death wasn't around the next corner? With my mindset poverty, it felt too daring to even dream of that.

My favourite activity, by far, was anything to do with stories. Reading, writing, acting – anything where I got to live someone else's life, even just for a short while. The storybooks from my previous life at my nan's house quickly disappeared into the bottomless pit of my parents' beer money kitty, adding books to the list of things missing from my home life. So my eyes lit up when Mr Williams announced that the school was setting up a book club and we were each issued with a card.

The idea was we bought a stamp each week and when we had enough stamps, we got a book. I regularly stole coins from my biological mother's purse to buy sugar-filled sweets to keep hunger at bay at the weekends, but even I knew that books were a luxury we couldn't afford. By the time my classmates were busy handing over their full cards and choosing their books, my card had a grand total of – let me see now – no stamps at all.

Undeterred by my lack of financial resources, I went to the book club anyway. I loved hanging around the shelves on wheels after school once a week. In addition to providing an extra hour in a space for Paul and I to be in that was safer than home, I loved to open, read and even smell the new books. Yes, smell! Oh, that new-book aroma.[2] Back then, it was such an extraordinary treat to have a brand-new book in my hand and I savoured everything I could about it.

To get into the after-school book club, you had to show your stamp card, which was folded in half, with your name printed on the front and the stamps on the inside. Every week mine would be opened, checked for stamps (still zilch) and returned to me. I simply put on my 'don't care' mask and ran straight into the hall. One night, however, the woman on the desk opened my card and said, 'Wow, it looks like you can finally buy a book tonight.' Confused, I seized the card and almost stopped breathing when I saw enough stamps to buy not one but two whole books!

I had no idea how they got there, and rationalised that there must have been some mistake or that someone must have broken into Mr Williams' desk (he kept the cards locked in the top drawer) and, for some reason, stuck a load of stamps onto a random card. It could happen. It was only later that I worked out it must have been Mr Williams himself. He'd invested his own money in me and stuck the stamps in there, avoiding an embarrassing conversation during which he

---

2   Go on, give it a go – sniff this book. Smells good, no?

would have offered me charity and, insulted to the core, I would have fiercely declined.

Pushing away the guilt of using the stamps I hadn't paid for I decided to spend them. I rationalised that I'd give them back after a few precious hours – maybe even a couple of days. For a few precious moments I'd have my own book in my own hands. I grabbed the two books I'd been reading/smelling for the past few weeks and took them to the desk: one was a storybook guide to origami, and the other was my favourite book of all time, *The Turbulent Term of Tyke Tiler* by Gene Kemp. These two books were my closest friends, and I guarded them with my life, reading and rereading (smelling and re-smelling) them again and again.

Partly because I couldn't believe my luck having two of my own books, and partly because I expected someone to take them away any minute, I kept my books with me at all times. I took them to school in the day and at night I hid them under my bed, moving them to a different part of the mattress every night so they wouldn't be found and sold. They brought a sliver of light into the darkness of my homelife and I would have run into a burning building to save them.

I managed to keep those original copies close to me through multiple foster care placements, community houses and four years of sofa surfing during university. I still have the original copies today and have read Tyke's story to my own children. More than simply works of literature, and with no adult invested enough to save any of my own work brought home from school, these two books, along with the few photos I have of me growing up when I lived with my nan, were my treasure. A handful of material objects that prove I existed.

Good girl

Mr Williams had an annoying habit. He would insist on dragging over anyone who came into the classroom to stand by one of us and show off in his lilting Welsh accent about how brilliant we were.

'This kid is great! I'm so proud of her effort today.'

'She's worked so hard to keep it together and focus today.'

'Read this story she's written, it'll blow your mind!'

At first, it bamboozled me. Who would care about the tiny positives in our class when there were so many glaringly obvious negatives? After a while, though, there was a definite shift in class culture, a change in our learning-to-rioting ratio, and we spent more time engaged in our education rather than fighting to resist it. This slow but steady transformation meant we ended up with even more visitors and on some days our classroom resembled Piccadilly Circus. Everyone who came in got the lowdown from Mr Williams on how amazing we were.

One phrase I hated back then was 'good girl'. Still do. My stepfather would say it after raping me. 'Good girl.' Whenever I heard it at school, apart from making me feel physically sick, it felt lazy – the sort of thing someone says when they aren't really paying attention or can't be bothered to get into specifics. Proper Category 2 material.

Mr Williams, on the other hand, was all about specifics. His language was dripping with description. 'I love the way you stuck at that experiment' or 'Using that basket was clever thinking' or, my personal favourite, 'You've used that vivid imagination of yours there'. He wrote about my vivid imagination in my school report and I showed anybody and everybody – the lollipop lady, Raj the newsagent, the woman who helped me when I dropped the washing all over the floor at the launderette. I read it to my brother and kept the report folded up in my sock. The only thing I didn't do was show it to my parents. Not only was it dangerous to attract any kind of attention from them, but I wanted to keep the power of those words alive and safe from ridicule or the bin. Sitting alone and reading them silently to myself felt like being injected with undiluted hope.

Mr Williams was a one-man powerhouse, clearly on a mission to get us to believe in ourselves when that couldn't have been further from our minds. He looked for whatever it was we excelled in and then used it as leverage to stretch our engagement and learning. Standard, inspirational *Dead Poets Society* stuff, I hear you cry. With a teacher who chooses to be human first and professional second and commits to meeting children where they are, of course children are going to succeed. It's what great teachers are always focused on and do naturally.

You see, when things got really bad at home, Mr Williams' passionate investment in my success was sometimes too disconcerting for me to bear. That disconnect felt like torture. Life at home meant I already knew the truth about me (according to the adults there) – I was a dirty, worthless, guilty, black b*tch whose job was to clean, look after my three brothers and protect my parents from the rest of the world finding out what they were doing to me. The evidence was plain to see. Sure, school was a place where I could get lost in a book or excel at being someone else in the latest play, but none of that was real, was it? I loved the time spent in Mr Williams' ACE[3] classroom but felt like the contract was broken at the end of every day. In my young mind, Mr William's pants were well and truly on fire.

The disconnect between home and school

For kids navigating my kind of chaos, home and school are two very different beasts. You're basically Robin Williams at the end of *Mrs Doubtfire*, running back and forth between two places and trying to remember to be the right person in each. The gulf of disconnect in values between the home and school causes massive internal conflict. Have a read of that sentence again.

At home, the abuse continued daily. Success was staying invisible, trying to hide alcohol so my parents didn't get too drunk and pretending to be asleep when my stepfather came into my room at night. I regularly failed on every count.

With no other option than to accept victim status, evenings, weekends and half-term holidays meant functioning under the weight of darkness and despair. When I was allowed to attend school, everything about my existence was upgraded because of one simple truth. At school, I was valued.

Reading this you might conclude that at least children have somewhere to come and be normal, to escape and be a child. You'd be correct – partially. But (and it's a mahoosive one) remember that disconnect I mentioned? The state of overdrive your brain has to reach in order to maintain two completely different and totally opposed states of 'truth' really messes with your sense of self, reality and wellbeing. Whenever the elastic became too overstretched, I broke.

School encouraged me to have confidence in myself, to revel in self-worth, to embrace challenges and to make mistakes. At home, this mindset would be audacious and reckless. All were strategies that would earn me a beating.

---

3   Before I'd heard of ACEs (adverse childhood experiences) I used the same acronym to describe the relationships my Everyday Heroes built with me. **A**uthentic, **C**onsistent and **E**mbedded with high **E**xpectations.

School promoted kindness, tolerance and the use of descriptive adjectives in writing that would draw unwanted attention if I attempted to use them at home.

I had little choice but to live two lives, each aimed at keeping the Category 1 and Category 3 adults in my life happy. Put simply, happy Category 1 adults were persistent and powerful rays of warm sunshine. Happy Category 3 adults were just about drunk and/or high enough to be too preoccupied to notice me. The daily dissociation this required of me made living separate lives increasingly impossible as I progressed through school. For those precious six hours a day (excluding weekends, half terms, Easter, Christmas and summer) I could experience life at the lower, more palatable level of DEFCON Level 3 rather than my usual essential alert state of Level 1.[4]

When school finished, I had to take the long walk back home, during which the tar in the pit of my stomach re-solidified and grew heavy. Free school meals were replaced with empty plates. Kind words of encouragement gave way to a stream of verbal abuse. Helping hands were traded for violence and exploitation. Life. Was. Exhausting. My anger and self-hatred began to leak out – not at home where it could get me killed – but in the only place that was safe to speak out – school.

Undercover mother

From September to April, it was colder inside our house than outside. Paul and I would wake early with frozen hands and feet. We would assess how cold it was going to be that day by doing what we called 'The Dragon Test' – breathing and seeing if the early morning air was sharp enough to freeze the water droplets in our breath so it was visible.

The only source of heat in our house was an old coal fireplace downstairs in the front room. I learned how to light a fire in the fireplace by filling the grate with screwed up newspaper and, in the absence of Yuletide winter logs to burn,

---

4   DEFCON Level 3 is defined as 'increase in force, heightened readiness' and Level 1 is 'nuclear war is very soon or has already begun'. 'Heightened readiness' accurately describes my anxiety and fear-driven state of being. I wish I had the words to explain to the adults in school what I was operating under and why remembering to bring a green pen for French might simply be not at the top of my agenda, rather than the premeditated act of war it appeared to be.

adding bits of furniture, fabric or cushion filling from whatever we had fished out of the skip.

My curiosity and desperation were bigger than any fear of fire and I experimented to find the quickest route to chilblain-free warmth. I found that if I wedged our wooden-handled metal dustpan between the grate and the top of the fireplace I could fashion a central post that allowed me to spread a large sheet of newspaper across the open space. I quickly worked out that creating a vacuum in the chimney enabled the fire to blaze more quickly and gave me a few precious seconds to add more substantial fuel.[5] Often the paper would catch fire and I would have to act quickly to put the flames out before it flew onto the sofa and set it alight. I was driven more by what my parents would do if they saw scorch marks than the actual house burning down.

I was frustrated by the burden of having to be responsible for my baby brother, but at the same time had an unrelenting impulse to protect him. Back at nan's house, when he was younger, he had been a mild annoyance, but since we'd moved in with my parents, I had levelled up from sister to full-time child-parent and I wasn't even very good at actually keeping him safe. I knew Paul needed more parenting than I could give and felt guilty about letting him down as a poor substitute.

Paul was small and didn't seem to be getting any bigger. He couldn't run fast enough to escape my stepfather's beatings and was too little to fight back himself. Whenever my stepfather grabbed my brother by his arms, hair or clothes, Paul's eyes would dart immediately towards me, full of fear and in search of protection. Even without his silent pleas my stomach physically churned to see him on the receiving end of such violence, and the intense surge of injustice would compel me to jump in. I stood up for Paul in a way I didn't seem to be able to stand up for myself.

Every Sunday my stepfather left early for what he called 'work'. He cleaned windows with Uncle Mick, who hadn't let the fact that his bed and brothel had been smashed up and closed down by a rival entrepreneur deter him from branching out into burglary. Cleaning windows was a great way to see inside houses and work out which ones were the best to 'do over'. I knew that stealing was wrong, but I also benefited from the hot water boiled in the kettle that appeared without a box or receipt and clothes that had been taken from other people's washing lines. This added to my thoughts of worthlessness. I was a bad person who couldn't seem to do the right thing.

---

5   One of the reasons I was annoyed at flunking science in school. I may have failed to remember the elements from the periodic table but I excelled at what I called 'survival science' outside of school.

My stepfather would return home late morning with sausages and bacon and prepare a cooked breakfast for him and my biological mother. The smell of frying bacon was unbearable to Paul and me, and we must have become more of an annoyance as a new rule was established. Whatever the weather, we had to be out of the house before my stepfather got back from work until after the pubs closed. That was 10.30am at the latest until 2.30pm at the earliest. As much as we didn't want to be at home, trudging the streets in the freezing cold when you don't own a coat is as miserable as it sounds. As the next babies were born they joined the Sunday caravan and I became the eight-year-old defender of a six-year-old scaredy cat, a dribbling toddler and an ever-hungry crying baby.

At first, we stayed close to home, at the nearest park, checking every few minutes to see if anyone was back at the house. Once I adjusted to how long four hours actually was, and once more brothers were born, I pushed the huge heavy beast of our double pushchair, containing a baby and a toddler and made heavier by Paul riding on the back when his legs got tired, further afield. We walked for miles, standing in doorways when it was raining, and discovering new parks on the local estates. I taught the toddlers to scour the streets looking for dropped coins. Outside of pubs was the best place as people came out drunk, fumbling in their pockets for keys or bus fares, and dropped coins on the floor which they were too hammered to pick up. If we found ourselves with enough coins for actual food, I'd buy milk – the cheaper sterilised kind that was always left over at the newsagents. My beloved school adults relentlessly banged on about calcium making bones strong and my crazy plan, which made perfect sense to me at the time, was to grow my brother into an adult human male so that he could stand up to my stepfather and I could take a day off.

I parented my younger siblings as best as I could, struggling to do a job that wasn't mine and pushing the idea of being a child myself out of my mind.

The cost of compliance

Childhood transformed into a confusing and barren no-human land of suffering and survival. My parents alternated between ignoring Paul and me, beating us, and forgetting about us for days on end. There was never enough food and hunger was so constant that it went way past being debilitating to being simply boring. Our persistent state of hunger was so tiring and we were obsessed with finding food anywhere. Thank God for free school meals! Every lunchtime was a *Mission Impossible*-style event where I stuffed my pockets with scraps from my friend's plates to share with my brothers at home that night.

Having friends round to play, visiting someone else's house or attending a birthday party – the kind of experiences that my husband Ed and I have always prioritised for our own children to enjoy as part of their development as mini humans – were alien concepts. We were alone. As young humans navigating this kind of chaos typically do, I internalised the way I was treated as being somehow my fault. My brain needed to close the story loop left by so many questions about why this was happening to me. The quickest and easiest answer was that I was intrinsically bad and was inadvertently doing something to deserve the treatment I received.

Paul and I experienced two types of violent beating from my stepfather. One happened in response to an irritant, whether or not it had anything to do with us – his team losing at darts, running out of milk, coming downstairs to find the mess he'd left there himself when drunk the night before. Something would make him angry and he would lash out at whoever was near. This was a sharp slap from the back of his hand to the back of my head, one that would jerk you forward with sudden force. These beatings were impossible to avoid because it was a case of being in the wrong place at the wrong time. They were usually one slap and done, as long as you kept your mouth shut and didn't cry or answer back.

The other type of violence was much worse – premeditated punishment. These beatings seemed to be mainly reserved for me and could be psychological or physical. Both involved the use of his huge cowboy-buckle belt. Just seeing him remove it made a little bit of sick come up in the back of my throat.

These more terrifying beatings were preceded by my stepfather talking himself from a passive to an aggressive mood. He'd stalk me around the house, knowing I had nowhere to run, and then loom over me staring me down before the beating began. This tactic was effective and worked well for a year or so. As I got older I became used to the facial expressions and body language of adults when they switched from friend to foe. I spotted this in a variety of school adults trying to assert authority. I experimented with mirroring this behaviour back, in an attempt to discourage the inevitable violence by standing my ground. Ironically, at school this would be called 'challenging behaviour' when, to me, it was always defensive.

Or, as my stepfather called it: 'Defiance'.

The truth about lies

Life was made more difficult with the additional responsibility of a one-year-old and a baby to look after. I made bottles of watered-down milk, tried to distract them with stories and games and created a distraction whenever I saw my parents getting angry at either of them, which resulted in me being used as a punching bag in their place. My newest siblings were defenceless and, like all children, were programmed to seek out safety and connection. It killed me to see them cry and reach out their arms to my biological mother, only to see them be ignored or pushed away. They needed a parent, so I became one.

My heart softened towards Paul and hardened towards my parents whenever I saw how scared they made him feel. To this day I'm still physically unable to stand by and watch someone being violent towards someone else. Of course, being his big sister, I did boss him around, but he was my brother – and my closest confidante. We were united in the oppression we were under at home. He stood up for me without hesitation whenever I got into a tussle with another kid on the street. What was he supposed to do when an adult attacked him in his own home? I believed I deserved everything I got because believing I was worthless helped me to accept my fate. Paul being hurt was different. I had zero compassion for myself but saw adults hurting him as heinous and unforgivable.

Saying no to my stepfather was a guaranteed one-way ticket to punishment and pain. What might seem bizarre to anyone who is unaware of how humans, particularly children, tend to blame themselves for the trauma caused by others, was that I used this technique as a form of self-harm at school. I pushed kind adults wanting, no, needing, them to break and lash out at me, verbally or physically, it didn't matter – anything that would confirm that I was in fact dirty, worthless and guilty.

When I reflect back now, it's easy to see that my stepfather exhibited the vindictive behaviour of one attempting to seize the control he felt he lacked. This came out as racist and misogynistic verbal, physical and sexual abuse. He especially hated me intervening when he was being violent towards Paul and became more and more vindictive towards me. For example, pinning me down and dangling his lit cigarette over my arm. While the orange glow burned slowly, he would lean close, whisper into my ear and make me agree to statements I didn't fully understand.

Him: 'You're a filthy half-caste b*stard, aren't ya?'

Me (*in pain, under duress and swallowing the bubbling denial in my gut with my eyes never leaving the end of his cigarette*): 'Yes.'

Him: 'Say it!'

Me: 'I'm a filthy half-caste b*stard.'

Fortunately, my biological mother would intervene with specific pleas to my stepfather, 'Not the arms! Not the face!' She knew that visible marks would bring questions from social workers and school so any violence that could leave a mark tended to be focused on the stomach, back, tops of legs and chest. All the places on the human body which could be covered with clothing. Though there was the ever-present danger of this at weekends, school holidays were worse. The extra days away from school gave any wounds left by beating time to heal.

I knew what the adults in my life wanted. Total compliance. I knew it would be easier to just do whatever my parents at home and my teachers at school said. But even when it wasn't right? Even when I had not done anything to warrant being treated a certain way? I had an incredibly strong sense of injustice coupled with a very short fuse. When I was too afraid or weak to stand my ground, school got the brunt of my anger. In my safe place of sanctuary, where I was rarely grabbed, pulled, punched, or pinned down by adults, I had an outlet for trying to describe in words what I felt in my soul. Like *Hamilton*, my problem was that I had 'a lot of brains but no polish'. My over-the-top reactions to being told to remove my coat (when I was freezing cold) or stop running to the front of the lunch queue (when I was starving hungry) appeared disproportionate to adults. Adults expected more from me in the behaviour arena – which I would have gladly given if all my energy wasn't focused on navigating the shame, fear and exhaustion of unwarranted guilt at home.

So when teachers praised me at school it was impossible to hear. It was disconfirming data that actually made me feel sick. A 'truth' too powerful to hold.

Back to the out-of-body experience I described at the top of this chapter. Me, with my face held down in a saucer of wet bread and sour milk, alternating between trying to fight and failing before inevitably giving up.

Kneeling on the cold and stained lino, and too weak to fight back, the truth hit me like an anvil dropping out of the sky in a *Road Runner* cartoon. I felt a millisecond of gratitude as I realised the secret of life: 'There is no point.' That was the truth. There was literally no point in trying. I wasn't good enough and nothing I could do would ever be good enough. The last hope I'd held on to of being rescued drained out of my body.

So, no, Mr Williams. You're wrong.

You are, in fact, a liar.

I'm not going to 'do something great in the world'. Not at all.

This is me.

This is who I am.

This is *all* I am.

And this is all *I will ever be.*

I. Give. Up.

I stopped fighting, succumbed to the overriding weakness my body and mind felt and collapsed into the rancid mixture.

Take a minute to breathe. Not because it's comfortable but because this is important. What I've just described was not the end – it wasn't even a semi-colon let alone a full stop. Ready? Let's continue.

The moment I was rescued

After the milk incident, I was about as stable as an unexploded bomb. Life became more and more devoid of hope. At school, before then and despite my teachers' best efforts to encourage and engage me, my response was inconsistent. I was living with unprocessed and ongoing trauma and had to find a way of compartmentalising what I went home to every night in order to exist in school during the day. Without the words to verbalise my internal conflict, I frequently became frustrated and exhibited challenging safety-seeking behaviour.[6] Most of all I wanted to be seen rather than ignored and, like an addict, I settled for any attention, even negative, being better than none at all.

Thanks to enormous Victorian pipes that weaved in and out of every classroom, my primary school was always toasty warm. I loved curling up next to the heated pipes to listen to a story or complete an activity in relative peace and quiet. For a child who was familiar with hunger, free school meals were a literal life-saving element – pudding made me feel like royalty!

The adults in my school built relationships with me and I slowly began to trust some of them. I joined after-school clubs which meant I could enjoy playing netball, singing in a choir and discovering I was brilliant at origami.

Paul and I hung around even after the after-school clubs were finished. We developed several tactics and stories to manipulate the adults into letting us stay, including pretending to look for a lost coat in the upstairs hall until it was time for the school to be locked. Even then I would have happily slept in the library. One evening the caretaker noticed us and called us over. We got chatting and he made us two mugs of tea (strong enough to dissolve a lung) and let us have a go on the huge Zamboni-like machine that buffed the parquet floors of our hall! What he lacked in health and safety knowledge, he made up for in compassion and kindness. One thing I knew for sure about my primary school was that from midday supervisors to the receptionist, from the site manager to the head teacher, it was the closest thing I had to a real family.

I'd been off ill all week after the milk incident, but I was finally starting to feel better and looking forward to the safety of a roomful of rebels laughing at Mr Williams' moustache. On the Sunday night before I was due to return, we were sitting in the front room. My brother and I sat at the skip-chic glass-with-a-crack-topped coffee table with the younger ones nearby while my parents sat behind us on the sofa, dinner plates balanced on their knees.

During mealtimes, we had all learned that it was safer to be 'seen and not heard' so I always kept my head down, my eyes bowed. On this occasion, there was a cowboy film on the TV and the gunfights attracted my attention. 'Oi, you little b*tch, eyes down!' shouted my stepfather from behind me. I didn't flinch. I was used to being shouted at – which is why I rarely flinched when a teacher raised their voice in school.

When my head lifted to look at the TV for a second time, I heard my stepfather's plate crash to the floor. Before I could turn to see what was happening, my

---

6   Words matter. Swapping 'This child has challenging behaviour' for 'I find this child's behaviour challenging' shifts the focus from labelling the child to acknowledging our own response – a subtle change in words that opens the door for a little more possibility.

head was smashed forward at an alarming rate by the force of his hand. I bounced off the corner of the coffee table and my back hit the floor. It took a few seconds for the shock to subside and the pain to register. I felt blood dripping down my cheek and heard my biological mother screaming, 'Not the face! Not the face!' I lay on the floor as the sharp pain throbbed louder than the noise from the room, vaguely aware of my brother crying, gravy dripping onto my legs, and my parents screaming at my brother and the babies, who were all crying, to be quiet.

My stepfather reached down and grabbed my spindly body by my arm. Lifting me to my feet like a pile of laundry, he dragged me over to the cellar door and thrust me towards it, screaming at me to get out of his sight. Knowing he meant the cellar but desperate not to spend another night, having been forgotten about and left down there, I took a chance and ran past the door to the back room. I stumbled upstairs as fast as I could, pulling my sleeve over my hand to hold it up to my eye and stem the bleeding. Once in my room, I collapsed face down onto my mattress, holding my throbbing eye and listening to the muffled screams of my biological mother shouting at my brother to pick the food off the floor as I convulsed with sobs.

I knew I'd be kept home from school for another week to give the black eye time to heal but, having been ill the week before, I was desperate to get back to the place that I lived for. Mr Williams' pants may have been on fire, but his lies were still a whole lot more palatable than my truth.

I remember this incident as being unlike other similar beatings. It was the catalyst that convinced me to accept that life was hopeless. However, this fact somehow caused a monumental shift. I let go. I no longer cared what happened to me anymore, what my parents might do to me if I disobeyed them, and it made me feel slightly invincible.

I was done with living two lives, keeping the secret of what my parents did for fear of them getting into trouble and what they would do to punish me. If I disobeyed my parents and went to school, they would be sure to beat me, withhold food, lock me in the cellar and maybe finally fulfil their longstanding threat/promise to kill me. So what if they did? If this was life, I was done with it anyway. Though I couldn't verbalise it at the time there was something strangely liberating about the fact that I couldn't win – that I would never win, no matter what I did. This was a game set up for me to lose and when you're in that position, the only thing left to do is move the goalposts and play a game you have a chance of winning. So I chose to do the one thing that winning was for me – escape my home and take myself to school.

Waiting until my stepfather had left for work the next day, I changed the babies' nappies, gave them some milk, grabbed Paul and darted through the front door to freedom. I could hear my biological mother shouting for me to stay put, but I ignored her and raced towards the lollipop lady who was stationed on the main road. Her usual bright smile faded when she saw my face. I had a large cut that had not been attended to, other than me holding the sleeve of my jumper over it, and an enormous bruise that was still reddish-brown with an orange and yellow tinge at the edges. I looked exactly like a child whose face had been smashed against a glass-topped coffee table.

'What in God's name av ya done to ya face, girl?'

Instinctively, my hand went up to cover it. There were no mirrors in our house, so I had only seen myself in the reflection in the window at night. After every attack, once my stepfather had calmed down, he'd remind me, 'If anyone asks, ya fell, alright?' I couldn't work out who was more stupid – my parents for believing they could get away with it or the adults who seemed satisfied with such a clear deception.

Still not able to transfer my bravery to words, I trotted out my well-rehearsed response, 'I fell.' The look on her face told me she didn't believe my explanation. Rather than being scared that I hadn't been believed, I felt relieved. If she had just accepted my answer, I would have had to downgrade her from a Category 1 Everyday Hero to a Category 3 idiot. I knew she didn't believe me and that was enough. She couldn't do anything to stop the pain I felt but she could stop traffic and get me to school.

The looks I was getting from the parents dropping off their children – and from the kids themselves – alerted me to the fact that this black eye was not something anyone could miss. I dropped my brother off in the bottom playground and ran to hide in the toilets near my classroom. That's when I saw my face for the first time and when the last shred of any dignity withered. I'd been a fool – my two separate worlds of home and school were about to collide for the first time, and I had no strategies for coping with the impending explosion.

The bell that signalled the start of the day signalled the start of the questions.

> **Kid in toilet:** 'Urgh, your face, what av ya done?'
>
> **Me:** 'I fell.'
>
> **Kid in corridor:** 'Wow, how did you get that shiner?'
>
> **Me:** 'I fell.'
>
> **Kid in classroom:** 'Had a scrap with a lamppost, have ya?'

Me: 'I fell.'

Previously I'd used humour to divert attention, coming up with a comic retort like, 'I had a knife fight with a shark!' The goal was to shift attention from my shame. This time I had nothing left in me other than lies and despair.

By the time I got to my classroom, everyone was staring and whispering. I sat at my desk wearing the second-hand bomber jacket that one of the midday supervisors had fished out from the lost property box and adopted the archetypal hood up/head down 'too cool for school' position children navigating the kind of chaos I've described are brilliant at. This was a new low. Now everybody knew. They could all see my shame, there was nowhere to hide and I had no idea what to do next.

When Mr Williams called the register, I kept my head down and didn't answer my name. I had literally run out of ideas for survival and sat on my chair staring down at the desk, my mind blank about what to do next. Maybe this was it? Maybe I would lose the will to live right there. Maybe I'd die at the same desk I'd written hope-fuelled stories of life and possibility.

Mr Williams set the class off on a task – probably something to do with dragons – before coming over and kneeling down beside me so that I could just about see him out of the peripheral vision of my one good eye. I still had my head down and was trying to stop myself from crying and giving myself away. His arm rested on the table behind me and I could see the frizz of his hair and imagined his moustache near my head. Part of me wanted to hug him and cry, but that would show weakness. And weakness spells danger. Letting adults know you were vulnerable was simply inviting betrayal. Or worse. So we sat in silence, me waiting for him to get fed up and leave and him determined to stay.

Eventually, he broke the silence by talking about my brother. I suspect he was hoping that the mention of his name might help open up a dialogue. To be fair, it usually did, but on that day I was swallowed up by wretchedness – I was broken. Even my reason for existing – to look after my brother – wasn't enough to pull me back into a place where I could even start to think about giving a toss.

After a few unanswered questions, he asked me the big one – 'What happened to your face?'

The dilemma he put me in made me angry. This was a make-or-break moment and the last thing I needed was yet another adult who I thought might be half-decent proving to me they were an idiot. If I lied, and he believed me, that would mean demoting him to a Category 3 and that would be the end of our relationship. If I told him the truth, there was also a risk that he would agree with my parents, that I was worthless and that I deserved everything I got. Worse still, what if he told them I'd snitched? Then I would have signed my own death warrant.

I hesitated. Everything Mr Williams had done, all of my interactions with him up to this point, indicated that he was a Category 1 adult. But he was a liar, wasn't he? What if everything he did was just one big confidence trick? In my experience, adults played tricks all the time. They tried to fool you by pretending to be nice, like buying you a colouring book, or holding your hand in public and then beating you and forcing you to do unspeakable things in private. It was too much. I had masses of hard-won evidence to prove to me that adults didn't give a toss, all of it now stacked up against one slightly sweaty and overly hairy adult crouching next to me who, weirdly, seemed to care. Decision time. I knew I had to say something. But what?

'I fell.'

Trust was too big a risk.

He asked me to look at him and I gingerly lifted my head. I was trying to throw him my best 'Get lost' look but was hampered by a bruised and swollen cheek moist with tears. His lips tightened and he stared me straight in the eye. He managed to deliver his next words with a steady calmness, even though he must have been losing it inside.

With his lilting Welsh accent, he said kindly but firmly, 'I don't think you fell. I think you're protecting someone. And what you need to know is, I'm here to protect you. I'm here to look out for you.'

His words entered a new and unfamiliar part of my brain. It was a space beyond and outside of the darkness at the heart of me. It was as if a fist had plunged inside my chest, reached the locked safe containing my dirty secret, brushed it aside as if it didn't matter, and carried on, deeper into my soul, deeper than anyone had gone before, deep enough to be able to gently touch the core of who I was as a human child.

I lowered my head so he wouldn't see me crying but he just carried on speaking, insisting that he would be here all day and I could talk to him whenever I was ready. I wanted to tell him everything there and then, everything. The pain, the beatings, the loneliness, the abuse, the shame. All of it. But this lifeline was all too much for me and I just sat hunched, my head down and my shoulders shaking as the sobs overtook me. I just didn't have the words.

Mr Williams showed his true Category 1 credentials. He was clearly in no rush and he didn't call for me to be removed from the class so he could just 'get on'.

He let me stay at my desk while the children worked around me. It was comforting to be in familiar surroundings and at morning break time, when the classroom emptied leaving only me, Mr Williams remained at his desk. I could hear him sorting out the pens in his pencil tin, the one with the Welsh dragon on it. Then he began to peel open his squashed cellophane-wrapped sandwiches and asked if I liked fish paste. I didn't even know fish came in paste but the offer was inviting and the promise of food was tempting. When I was sure we were alone, I walked warily over to him. Was I brave enough to say something?

I had worked out by then that if I did speak, there was no way I could tell him everything, much as I would have liked to. I had never spoken such words out loud and, besides, it was all my fault anyway, wasn't it? I mean, sexual abuse, rape, that sort of thing, I'd been told enough times. I deserved it all because I'd accepted what I'd repeatedly been told. That I was a black b*stard. That I was dirty. That I was worthless. The weight of the shame made it impossible for me to speak about that particular horror. However, I knew hitting someone was wrong. If I only shared the stuff I suspected might be against the law, then Mr Williams wouldn't blame me for that. I decided to tell him a little of my truth, just to see how he got on with it.

'My stepfather hit me. He hits me a lot. He hits my brother too.'

Those were the last few words I ever said to him.

As I spoke, I could see his face take on a new expression, one I'd never seen before. Not the I'm-furious-but-not-really-have-a-look-at-my-dancing-moustache face, but one of genuine red-hot indignant anger. Actually, it was something beyond anger. He looked like he was about to strangle someone with his bare hands. For a moment, I thought his fury was aimed at me and I panicked, wondering if I had read the situation wrong. I froze, waiting before he interrupted the tornado of thoughts in my mind with the last sentence he would ever say to me, one that would change everything:

'Go and get your brother.'

It wasn't only what he said but the way he said it, as if he were holding back some great torrent of emotion. The force of this emotion alone lifted me out of my chair and carried me down the hall to my brother's classroom. His teacher simply handed him over, looking at me in a strange way. On our way back to my classroom, we were met by Mr Williams in the corridor. He signalled that we should turn around and follow him and he quickly marched past us towards the library. Once there, he checked it was empty, ushered us through the door and shut it behind us, remaining outside.

After a while, the head teacher arrived. He talked to Mr Williams, who was standing with his back to the door and who I could tell was agitated from the way his arms and hair were flying around, not to mention the look on the head's face as he listened to what Mr Williams was saying.

My brother kept asking me what was going on. I told him I didn't know and I gave him some books to distract him while I crept up to the glass door to investigate. Mr Williams still had his back to the door, but I could see that he had acquired a cricket bat from somewhere, presumably the PE cupboard down the hall, and was slapping it repeatedly into his hand. What on earth was he doing with a cricket bat? Then it struck me – he was on guard duty. He was a knight. He was there to protect me from dragons. As if I was a princess in one of the stories he read us.

I was suddenly enveloped by a long-lost feeling from my distant past, a feeling I could only dimly remember. Was it safety? Relief? Humanity? I sat in that library and felt the sweet mixture of all three. Mr Williams had put his money where his moustache was and was standing outside the library. It wasn't the rescue that registered. It was the fact that he stood for me – he stood up, he stood out, he stood there. That's the definition of what Everyday Heroes do, isn't it? They stand.

Adults came and went but Mr Williams never left his post outside that door. Eventually, a woman turned up who I guessed was a social worker (she was wearing the wrong shade of brown – a dead giveaway in the 1980s). The head came into the library and gently explained that this lady was going to take us somewhere safe, where we would be looked after. This threw up a million questions and I glanced fearfully towards the door, only to see Mr Williams, cricket bat in hand, slowly nodding and encouraging me to accept the news.

A nod from Mr Williams was good enough for me. I slipped into parent mode, took my brother's hand, and told him to leave the books and come with me. The social worker smiled and took his other hand and the three of us walked out of the library and towards her car. I had no idea what would happen next, but I trusted Mr Williams. Turns out he wasn't a liar. It was me who had been too scared to tell the truth. Now I had and things could change for the better as a result. I trusted him so much that I didn't even look back. I didn't know it then, but that would be the last time I would ever see the Weirdo from Wales.

Mr Williams' Legacy

The Victorian heating pipes surge warmth into my palm as I stand in my childhood classroom. The years that have passed dissolve and I am eight years old again, pressed against the pipes, stomach growling, remembering Mr Williams guarding that library door with his cricket bat.

When a filmmaker suggested making a film about my childhood and the impact teachers had on my life, my first thought was: I would have to go back to my old primary school. By some bizarre turn of events, the head turned out to be someone I trained to be a teacher with! The two days we spent in my hometown were equally harrowing and healing but culminated in the time travelling experience of being back in the love and safety of my old primary school. I had the honour of working with the children there and you can see the compelling, tear-jerking and celebratory result, asserting teachers as Everyday Heroes, in the finished film, *Re-Story Your Life*.[7]

I sat in my old classroom, in the same seat, next to where the sink met the huge Victorian pipes, got to sit in the head teacher's chair (!) and led a session with a class of wonderful eight-year-olds. Their teacher met them with a smile and that precious gift of being seen. One boy caught my eye – surrounded by children taller than himself, he looked tired. When the teaching assistant asked him a question, he seemed not to hear. She didn't hesitate. Instead, she knelt beside the desk and spoke softly. Slowly, the boy's shoulders relaxed. I recognised that moment – and knowing the legacy power of that simple act made my heart swell with emotion.

My connections with the adults in my primary school were the closest thing I had to family relationships. I saw them every day, we knew each other's ways and laughed with (or at) each other. Young humans are conditioned to seek out nurture and school is where I found it. In short, I loved school because school loved me first.

---

7   Details on my website: https://jazampawfarr.com.

Primary school met me where I needed to be met: the luxury of free hot food every day school was open[8] and a variety of after-school clubs which gave us an extra hour of security and reassurance from the adults who ran them. Long before breakfast clubs were a thing, a dinner lady came in early to make tea and toast for anyone who turned up before the gates officially opened. That incentive alone played a huge part in my opting to stick with school rather than roam the streets looking for food to steal. I made sure to get myself and Paul up and dressed and into school promptly every day.

Whether you spend time with young people as an educator, a health professional, shopkeeper, coach, or just a neighbour, you can make a compassionate connection with a child. Some of the adults who laughed with me, joked with me, showed me kindness or offered me a sandwich (or let me run around a school hall, willy-nilly, with a potentially dangerous piece of industrial cleaning equipment) had no understanding of the complexity I existed in at home and they didn't let that stop them.

Statistically, I should be dead, in prison, or lost to exploitation. Instead, I'm standing on stages worldwide, reminding people about the power they have to transform lives. To be human first.

Mr Williams taught me that truth is more than mere facts – it's about seeing someone's value even when they can't see it themselves. He stood guard with that cricket bat not because he could fix everything, but because he refused to let fear win. He chose to be Category 1 when Category 2 would have been far simpler – and was the extent of his job description.

If your work involves fighting for the highest good of young people, please take care of your greatest resource – yourself. I know you're exhausted. I know the system feels impossibly restrictive, but you are creating a legacy with every act of with-ness. You move the needle a little every time you choose to believe in a child who doesn't believe in themselves. That belief doesn't have to be perfectly formed. It just needs to be big enough to allow you to be present.

Your students may never return to tell you how you changed their trajectory. But I'm telling you now – your work changes lives. I am living proof of that. This is how my story becomes *our* story, and by the time you finish this book it goes on to form *your* story. In short, the truth Mr Williams taught me is that

---

8 You can't teach the bus stop method for long division to a kid dealing with the constant hollow ache of hunger. The first thing I did when I got my own class was to stock the cupboard with crackers, jam and illegal rich tea biscuits because no one was ever going to feel how I had felt. I've come across a handful of schools that have committed to staying open 365 days a year and persuade local businesses to work with charities so that children relying on free school meals – and their families – can eat during the holidays, weekends and half terms. Stick a food bank in the staffroom – for staff and families. It's not your job and you shouldn't have to even think about it. Do it anyway.

sometimes the fiercest act of revolution is simply showing up, day after day, refusing to let the dragons win.

That's Everyday Heroism.

And you're already doing it.

With or without the use of a cricket bat.

Be Mr Williams: Reflections

If you've experienced anything like I've described in this chapter, please head to the back of the book where you'll find a section addressing you personally and a series of places you can access help and support.

1. **Meet people where they are**

    The most powerful connection happens when we meet people as they are, not where we need them to be. Mr Williams looked behind the front to see the me underneath. On the surface I was a defensive and distrusting kid. Remind you of anyone? Who in your life might need you to look behind their front to see what they're really carrying?

2. **Purchase a comparison cactus**

    Mine's called Dave. He's a prickly and unforgiving little fellow who sits on my desk and reminds me not to fall into the comparison trap! This isn't the Disadvantage Olympics. Your trauma is valid whether it was 'as bad as' someone else's or not. How can you honour both your own struggles and those of others with compassion and without comparison? Remember, healing is not a competitive sport.

3. **Embrace the three Es: Empathy, Engage and Enrol**

    Mr Williams used what I call the three Es to create meaningful change and connection and gain my trust before challenging my worldview. Starting with an emphasis on seeking to understand, by swapping jumping to judgement for getting curious. Then draw people into a conversation by listening first and, finally, actually inviting them to change their behaviour. If there's no foundation of safety and belonging, 'tough love' is just another form of rejection.

4. **Be human first (and professional second)**

   Your credentials aren't important to a child who just needs compassion. You don't need a degree in psychology to stand with someone – or, as Mr Williams proved, a decent haircut. You just need to lean into your humanity. Look to the world of business – in our digital age, leaders that create psychological safety through trust, hope and compassion are already winning. How might leading with your heart actually make you more effective in your role?

5. **Expand your garden of possibility**

   Just as physical poverty can limit access to resources, mindset poverty restricts belief in anything beyond what you have experienced so far. Mr Williams encouraged me to think of alternatives to my 'everyone dies' story endings. Where in your life are you still clinging onto a fixed mindset and letting fear drive your bus? What's one area where you could expand your vision of what's possible for yourself or the younger people around you?

6. **Build ACE relationships**

   Before anyone was using the term ACEs (adverse childhood experiences), Mr Williams created what I identified as an ACE relationship. One that was **A**uthenticity, crammed full of the **C**onsistency I craved and **E**mbedded with high expectations. Consider your relationships – especially with children and young people – and give yourself a score for each of the three elements. What small thing could you do to improve on your lowest score?

7. **Mind your language**

   Whether you're describing yourself or someone else, the words you use make a huge difference. Swapping 'This child has challenging behaviour' for 'I find this child's behaviour challenging' shifts focus from labelling the child to acknowledging our own response. What subtle language shift could open more possibility for a child you're struggling to connect with?

8. **Speak your truth**

   Mr Williams had the courage to stand. He pushed past any discomfort to wrap words around the truth of what he saw. There are moments when telling the truth becomes an act of revolutionary care. What difficult truth might you need to speak to create positive change? Don't let fear be the thing that stops you. Sometimes you have to go with facts over feelings.

9. **Stand in the fire**

    Assume the best. In any situation, you really only have three choices: do something to make it better, do something to make it worse or do nothing at all. Two of them have a negative impact. The most powerful intervention is standing shoulder-to-shoulder with a child in turmoil and refusing to move. For the current chaos navigators in your life, how can you be present without trying to fix everything?

10. **Avoid reinforcing invisible barriers**

    Schools are under massive pressure to deliver – on attendance, outcomes, everything. But sometimes, in the drive to raise standards, we accidentally hold children accountable for their own disadvantage. Like rewarding pupils with 100% attendance with Easter Eggs in the end-of-term assembly. Not many six-year-olds are getting themselves up and driving themselves to school. Let's stick to rewarding students for things they actually have control over. Take a look at your policies, rewards and routines. Are they lifting barriers – or quietly reinforcing them?

Mr Simpson
The One Who Taught Me Consistency

I'm on stage looking out at the crowd of face-painted children and frazzled adults clutching a collection of balloons and half-eaten ice creams.

That's when I see him.

My hands freeze mid-air, and two of my three rainbow juggling balls drop to the ground. In that moment I was no longer Squiggle the Clown, I was a scared teenager wondering if I could ever be enough. The laughter from the crowd fades as realisation seeps in. Meanwhile, my fellow clown throws me a confused frown, wondering why I've stopped.

Mr Simpson.

He hasn't changed in ten years. Sleeves rolled up. Tie loose. I'd recognise that dishevelled geography teacher vibe anywhere.

He's standing with his wife being circled by two small children. I'm transported back to my regular walk of shame down the late corridor, Mr Simpson leaning on the wall and serving relaxed calmness that remained unchanged no matter what kicked off in the corridors.

That demeanour had once been a catalyst for change in my life. A quiet revolution caused by no grand gestures, just consistent kindness.

Before rational thought intervenes, I'm moving, leaping off the front of the stage. Still clutching my lone juggling ball, I hop, skip and stumble my way through a sea of theme park chaos, shouting with excitement.

'Mr Simpson!'

He looks over and sees me. No surprise. No shock. Not even a hint of panic as an unknown potential assailant dressed as Squiggle the Clown makes a beeline straight for him and his family.

Just that same steady gaze that once held me together when everything else was falling apart.

Life on the road

Some children collect rocks. Or stickers. Or football cards.

I collected survival strategies.

One thing I knew for sure was that adults were not to be trusted. Not all adults. Not most adults. But enough to make trust a luxury I could never afford.

Journeys to a new home in a social worker's car became familiar. Black plastic bags. Donated clothes that never quite fit. A childhood measured in temporary families, each trying to earn my trust, but none of whom I was with long enough to form a bond.

By eleven years old, my life had become a continuous shuffle between broken places – my parents' chaotic house and foster homes that felt like planets in a different universe. Each move reaffirmed the same brutal truth: something was fundamentally wrong with me. I was the problem. The reason no home was ever permanent.

All of my foster parents were kind people with kind intentions. I was the problem. They were exclusively middle-class and white adults whose world operated on different rules. Rules like eating together at actual tables, bedtime stories and creating and respecting safe boundaries. These concepts, though loving, were so foreign to me that I was constantly on high alert, waiting for the catch.

In one foster home, the catch turned out to be my new school. A school where being the only brown kid created first curiosity then animosity from the kids and straight-up othering from some of the adults. A particularly brutal moment: a well-meaning teacher declaring they 'didn't see colour' before lining me up with several of the popular kids and inviting the class to play spot the difference.

I learned a lot about survival during this time. I learned that education wasn't about perfect grades. It was about understanding yourself, learning to navigate a world that wasn't designed for you, and keeping your eye on the ultimate but impossible prize – transforming survival into something resembling hope.

Survival demands resilience. And resilience wasn't about being unbreakable. It was about shortening the time between being kicked to the ground and getting back up again. It's still a work in progress for me today. I have managed to reduce my bouncebackability from years of not trusting anyone to being able to reflect, reframe, pivot and go again in minutes – on a good day. Other days it takes longer, unfortunately. Both journeys are valid.

High School Musical

At eleven years old, I faced the grim trinity of being out of foster care, back with my parents and starting high school. Home was being policed by several Everyday Hero social workers who had been working with my parents while we were away. I couldn't get my head around why I was being returned to the care of adults who were not safe. I had a strong inkling that my social workers were as unhappy as I was with the arrangement, as they regularly dropped in for surprise visits.

For a while, my parents got drunk at home rather than leaving us unsupervised and unfed overnight. I was sent to my room for misdemeanours rather than the cellar. Even though I still stayed awake at night, staring at the door handle just in case, my stepfather temporarily stopped coming into my room at night. I stayed on alert, ready to run, and with my fingers crossed that the next time a social worker left our house, they'd take me with them.

High school brought new adults, new rules and exponentially more opportunities to mess up. The transition from primary to high school is a challenge for any eleven-year-old child, but even more so after the summer of no belonging – that six weeks when you don't belong to primary school anymore, but you don't belong to secondary school either.[1] I cycled between toxic states of fear,

---

1   I'm on the board of governors at my local high school which organises a sleepover for all the joining Year 6 kids. It's grown into an annual festival and, in addition to the usual transition events, has facepainting, camping and above average quantities of hot chocolate! It's neurodiverse friendly, the staff throw themselves into it and last year they even had a rather spiffingly coiffed therapy dog strolling around! Try it! You might lose a few Bunsen burners on the first go around but your kids feel a sense of belonging long before they turn up in September.

panic and a massive case of imposter syndrome. Within the first few days, I realised that none of my go-to strategies for surviving were going to be effective and felt like a spy in danger of being discovered at any minute.

By the time I ran screaming from the building five years later, my self-critical voice would have reached new heights in its self-destructive power.

My most pressing problem wasn't the academic work. I was smart and eager to learn. I was hugely motivated by a desire to distance myself from the example of adulthood I saw at home. Neither of my parents saw any value in academic pursuits and ridiculed my eagerness to attend school and actually do the work. I wanted something totally different to what they valued. I also desperately wanted to avoid adding to the ever-growing list of medals I kept unintentionally winning at the Disadvantage Olympics.

I appeared to be adept at getting things wrong. My English teacher laughingly explained that 'my face didn't fit' when I told him that I was good at acting and offered to play Mary in the Year 7 Nativity.[2] My history teacher advised with genuine kindness that if I 'just' behaved, thought, spoke and dressed differently, I might make something of myself. My religious studies teacher asked us what we thought happened after we died. My unfiltered and over-enthusiastic answer of 'You rot in your grave?' didn't go down well and was mistaken for blasphemy. I didn't know what blasphemy was, but what I learned that day was that doing it earned you a detention.

High school was a short, sharp shock of structure after a summer in residential foster care and the polar opposite of my primary school. Navigating the change was like being in a never-ending multi-layer platform game with no gold coins to collect and where you didn't get any points for beating the bad guys up. I was smart and keen and, on a good day, believed both of those things would help me to succeed. The kind of kid that thrives in education, right? Almost, but the ticket price set by this new collection of adults I hadn't known long enough to categorise yet was problematic. They wanted my compliance.

And not trusting them to easily hand that over was *my* problem, not theirs.

---

2   It was a Church of England school and every year the eleven-year-olds put on the Nativity for the governors and some big nobs in the church. It was nowhere near as cute as when five-year-olds dress up as mismatched shepherds in a school hall. Once my English teacher realised I was good at acting he cast me as Herod, because, while I'm clearly no Mary, my face was apparently the perfect fit to play a murderously male megalomaniac.

See me after school

My high school was red hot on obedience. Behaviour was everything and the more senior the adults, the more convinced they were that the students were one sandwich away from causing riots.

It was like those posters in train stations that start with the assumption that your sole purpose of catching a train is to start a fight with a ticket collector! The feeling was that we were on the verge of causing trouble and needed to be contained before that thought crystallised into an action.

All the adults in my life – at home and at school, apart from my five Everyday Heroes – insisted that I had to behave first and then, only then, could I belong. I desperately wanted to belong at school, but I wasn't interested in the roles I was given as the poor kid, the brown kid, the free school meals/pupil premium kid from the estate. In fact, the secret to the coveted prize of belonging appeared to be the same three Bs as my primary school but in reverse order. *'Behave'* in the way we decide is appropriate, *'Believe'* in the system we endorse and then, and only then, you can *'Belong'*. Outside of school, on the streets, non-compliance was what it took to get by, to eat, to keep me and my brother safe, again, to quite literally survive.

The first and most difficult hurdle was actually getting into the building. Success in this space meant surviving the morning 'welcome'. This consisted of those teachers who least felt the cold standing at the gate and berating students for their uniform infringements. It was less 'Great to see you' or 'Glad you made it in today!' and more 'Lengthen that tie!' or 'Take that hood down!' or 'That skirt's too short' or sometimes all three, always followed by, 'See me after school.'

Back at home, after a meeting (attended by no one advocating strongly enough for us kids) it was decided that my parents had made enough progress for social worker visits to cease. It didn't take long for the edges to fray, and things quickly returned to normal levels of neglect at home. In addition to dropping my brother off at primary school, I had to source clean clothes, find a way of masking the smell of urine from the previous night's bedwetting (to save you some time – without soap, there isn't one) and try to pull together something to eat.

Thanks to the social worker with the bright orange hair and a huge smile, we now had a fridge with its own freezer compartment. I was proud of my idea to scrape the ice from around the freezer door in the mornings and tell my brothers it was what Santa ate for breakfast.

Every day involved a series of anxiety-inducing difficult decisions. By the time I arrived at school most days, I was already exhausted. There was just no way I could arrive at high school on time after dropping my brother at our old primary school, so I went with what felt right and did the daily walk of shame down the late corridor.

Enter Mr Simpson – my form tutor. I had already begun to suspect he might be a Category 1 adult. He was often the first (often only) adult to actually smile and say hello to me in the morning. That tiny act of kindness and connection was either a clue or a trick. Mr Simpson always had his sleeves rolled up and his tie loose. He looked ever so slightly dishevelled as if to underline that teaching geography was really hard work.[3] You could usually spot him chatting to a disgruntled student in the corridor while leaning on the wall, all relaxed and comfortable in his own self – which baffled me entirely.

Every day I was late, Mr Simpson greeted me with a grin. 'Good to see you,' he'd say. 'You're here. Great. We can get started now.' Every single day. As if he was genuinely pleased to see me. The impact of his consistent kindness? It made me physically sick with rage. To me, it was disconfirming data that I absolutely did not deserve. However, sometimes that's how transformation starts. With a willingness to put aside yesterday's reaction and repeatedly saying hello for as many years as it takes for it to be heard.

In my first year, his kindness left me inexplicably confused and angry. During my second year, I tried harder to make him give up on me. By the third year, I started watching for him in that corridor!

Mr Simpson took the time to build trust. It took me a long time to learn how to let people show up for me without excessively testing their loyalty first. I'm still learning that if I'm honest. By refusing to give up even long after I already had Mr Simpson created a chink in my armour. When someone shows up like that every day for five years – every day for five years – it melts the ice around your heart.

---

3 Obviously, it is hard work because geography is a bona fide and integral curriculum subject! (Never diss a geography teacher – they know how to find you!)

The memo I missed

I was eager to learn but first had to navigate the unwritten rules of high school. I figured the specialist subject I could ace was resilience. I was a seasoned chaos navigator and knew that was one of those transferable skills. Unfortunately, school resilience was vanilla-flavoured and seemed to have been boiled down to achieving a couple of extra marks in a maths test. Getting yourself and your younger brothers up and dressed, distracting them from the absence of any available breakfast and delivering the school-aged one to their school on time didn't count. I was great at minty-choccy-chip-tutti-frutti flavoured resilience, but that just wasn't considered as valuable.

Survival at high school demanded I renounce everything I'd learned at home, where survival relied on compulsory acts of aggression. Ironically, outside of school, in the streets of my under-resourced community, the unwritten rules were much more obvious: if you want/need it and can't afford to pay for it then you take it. Appearing weak makes you a target so always get the first punch in. And the one I learned the hard way: being a child guaranteed being disrespected, ignored or manipulated by adults. Conforming to what felt like the nine-carat plastic school values left me exposed at weekends and during the holidays. The values were great but didn't work in my 'real' world outside of school. The stress of living two entirely different lives, constantly switching between conflicting rules of engagement, took an emotional and physical toll.

Not many of the other students seemed to find navigating high school culture as alien as I did. I was envious of those who arrived with pressed uniforms and new pencil cases – turning up in full student mode, having at least one adult at home who took care to make sure they were prepared and ready to learn. When asked why I had turned up to the lesson without anything to write with, I made the mistake of telling the truth – no one had given me a pen. The teacher tutted and launched into a tirade about me 'taking responsibility for my learning'. Responsible? Me? She didn't know the half of it and I wasn't very forgiving about her lack of understanding.

That isn't to say that schools shouldn't have values and vision and a belief in standards, of course, they absolutely should. The difficulty occurs when we assume (or the curriculum or the inspection framework assumes) that all students start from the same social and cultural norms. Simply expecting them to know how to behave or comply with rules without a shared understanding is, as my nan would say, 'hitting your head against a brick wall'.

In many ways, what I am talking about is the idea of social capital and there has been much made of this idea in recent years. I'm living proof that it is possible, but it's not as simple as slapping a couple of coats of middle-class paint[4] on every working-class kid! It relates to so many little things on a day-to-day basis, little things that add up. Social mobility comes at a cost, as it requires leaving a community behind – one that you can never return to as an insider again.

My problem was that I had absolutely no idea how to behave like a 'normal' student. I turned up at high school without the things my teachers assumed I already took for granted – like knowing they were on my side and that school was a safe place and when a male teacher got angry at me, it wouldn't result in the same violence as when my stepfather got angry with me at home. Few of the adults around me picked up on the signs of what I went home to every night. I was, after all, an expert in hiding them. The downside was that I had to take responsibility for things that were out of my control. The result meant being held accountable for my own 'disadvantage'.

Here's an example of how misplaced kindness can trigger an eruption. One of my teachers was keen on neat presentation – in our work and in our appearance. He liked to walk up and down the rows as we worked and examine the state of our nails. After repeatedly commenting on my general dishevelledness (and the fact that I slouched, which seemed to especially offend him) he instructed me to 'Ask your mum or dad to help you clean them if you can't do it yourself!' I scowled at him with a cocktail of anger, despair and shame. I didn't even own a toothbrush, and my parents only ever laid hands on me to hurt me, so why on earth would I invite them to touch me? Fixing my gaze on his bowtie, I concluded that we lived on different planets. His was one where parents had been nurtured themselves as children and experienced the necessary growth to pass that nurture on to their own. Apparently, in that world, no children were being abused by their carers, and bowties were compulsory attire for physics teaching. I spent my time in his class learning zero physics and finding the quickest way to get sent out of the lesson.

Depending on who was writing them, my school reports spoke of my 'disruptive nature' and 'lack of compliance' or the fact that I was 'a valued member of the class'. Those that singled out my negative qualities didn't offer any guidance on how I should evolve away from them. For me, expectations of compliance in high school and the focus on blind obedience to adults were too close to the powerlessness I experienced at home. There was no way I was going to even consider buying into it. It's not that I had a problem with authority *per se*, but I did have a problem with trust – and, you know, with good reason.

---

4 Available from Farrow and Ball. Google it. Made you look!

Here, I was being told what to do by people who simply assumed that I understood *why* I should trust them. Like any high school starter, I wanted to fit in. My problem was that I lacked the language to articulate those needs. I didn't even really know how to elicit a positive response from the adults in school.

All of this context shows why Mr Simpson's consistency mattered so much. He didn't demand trust before earning it. He didn't require me to be someone else before accepting me. He simply showed up, day after day, creating space for me to exist as I was, which, in time, changed the way I behaved.

Teaching starts with R (for relationship)

My biggest difficulty in moving from primary school to high school was the shift in staff–student relationships. High school was bigger and busier, with teachers who didn't seem to have as much time for smiling. It was difficult to get a read on my new school adults in order to categorise them.

Chaos at home meant I craved calm consistency elsewhere, so I warmed (slowly) to the teachers who I knew had a 'why' beyond just teaching their subject and controlling their students. The teachers who were compassionate made me feel like they valued my time and effort, and, in return, I responded by showing up and playing full out for them.

Mr Simpson didn't smile much. He had an expression that suggested he was waiting for something interesting to happen. There was a general consensus that Mr Simpson was an alien because he didn't blink. Despite that, Mr Simpson was the teacher everybody liked and one of the very few teachers I was bothered about being told off by. Spotting him sauntering down the corridor would be enough to bring any misbehaviour to a standstill, at which point he would nod in recognition and validation or stop for a chat. This was in contrast to the head teacher who opted to wear a cap and flowing gown and strode along the corridors with his hands behind his back, parting the student sea like Moses himself. Some of the braver delinquents from my primary school would stick two fingers up behind his back, which is probably where the similarity with Moses ends.

Mr Simpson rarely raised his voice. He didn't need to. Everyone, even the students who misbehaved in other lessons, was interested in what he had to say. I respected him, and when life got unbearably tough, he had invested enough in a relationship with me that I still tried hard to be a great student for him. I often failed, but I did try. And he seemed to know that. With my life coming apart at the seams and after having annoyed most of my other teachers to the point of no return, I kept waiting for Mr Simpson to join the other adults who I felt were against me. He never did. He appeared to be genuinely invested in me and refused to lose faith in me despite my many, many attempts to drive him away. It took years for me to even begin to grasp that loyalty doesn't always come with a catch.

As my form tutor, consistency was Mr Simpson's superpower. The stability this brought was vital. High school was too full on to be the break from the home turmoil that primary had been, so form time became my closest thing to family time. The conversations and culture he created made it safe for me to be and to belong.

Reading my old high school reports is a little bit heartbreaking. As a teacher myself, I've agonised over finding the right words and always insisted on writing them to the students rather than the parents. Reading the words of my teachers today objectively, you can see I wanted a connection but didn't know how to ask for it. They needed me to comply and were frustrated when I didn't. It's the perfect mixture of misunderstanding and lack of communication for a British sitcom. Phrases describing a 'lack of ability to apply herself' were the punchlines. I mean, c'mon. As if I would have survived long enough to be sitting in their lesson if I were actually lazy?[5]

Looking back, I wish more of my teachers had seen me the way Mr Simpson did. As an opportunity for them to do what they came into teaching to do – make a difference.

---

5   My favourite comment of all time was from my physics teacher, Mr H. 'This student would benefit from a lower physics set. Or even better still, no physics at all.' I applaud him for his honesty!

Crime and Punishment

High school meant the beginning of my five-year journey towards GCSEs, yet all the top grades in the world weren't going to be of any help to me with my limiting and fixed mindset that prevented me from believing in myself or feeling any sense of ownership of the successes I did pull off.

As a 'disadvantaged'[6] child, high school had the potential to provide me access to social capital and a wider world, a world that I had previously believed unattainable to me. Unfortunately, those five years mostly rubber-stamped my suspicion that I just wasn't good enough. Not because the adults I met didn't care, far from it, but because they were short on time in a system that was big on statistics. With the pressure to hit the targets and manage behaviour it's easy to see how zero tolerance can become the go-to.

On photo day, I was in school without a blazer, as usual. When I walked into the room where the photos were being taken, there was a pile of blazers on the table, guarded by a member of the senior leadership team who invited me to select one. Slipping into that blazer felt like I'd won the lottery! With a proper wool blazer, I could blend in! It felt like armour. I savoured the feel of it and, after the photo, got up to leave with a skip in my step. I barely made it to the corridor before a voice bellowed out across the hall, 'Return the blazer!' It wasn't the embarrassment of being called out in front of the rest of the students and the photographer that broke me that day. I punished myself for being so stupid as to believe I deserved the same as other students. I placed it back on the pile and walked back out to the corridor in shame.

Non-uniform days were even more of a challenge. I wore my school uniform, standing out even more than usual. Even if I could afford the payment, I didn't actually own any other clothes. The few I did have access to would have betrayed the poverty we lived in at home. Another unwritten rule I picked up was that being disadvantaged was a bad thing, and my job was to hide it from teachers and students. School uniform is meant to be a leveller but it can have the total opposite effect.

One of the most exciting things about starting high school is being let loose with a Bunsen burner. My physics teacher had given the class plenty of notice, along with the warning to remember to bring our lab coats in order to take part. I

---

6   I've asked leaders how their school refers to the children who are not disadvantaged. Two answers that stand out are 'the non-disadvantaged' and 'the normal ones'! See the Reflections section at the end of this chapter for some helpful suggestions on our use of language.

didn't have a lab coat but turned up to the lesson anyway, hoping there would be a spare I could borrow. I was rebuked for forgetting the one I didn't own and so had to sit out and watch my fire-starting peers having fun and trying to avoid losing their eyebrows.

I was already beginning to resign myself to the fact that I wasn't good enough. I received communications of simple rules that were meant to help keep order as evidence and data that I wasn't enough. I hated it, but I didn't disagree. In my keynote speaking, I ask people to raise their hand if they've ever felt like they weren't good enough. My hand is always the first one up! I still feel like this today and the battle with the belief that I am good enough is not one that I win every time.

I understood why my teacher made me sit out. He had made it clear to us in the previous lesson if we forgot to bring our lab coats, we wouldn't be able to do the lesson. I didn't even own a winter coat, let alone a lab coat. But I simply didn't have either the language or the courage to explain that I didn't have one to forget, and there was no way my parents could or would buy me one.

Week after week, I would sit out during every single practical lesson. Each time I withdrew to my stool in the corner, a little piece of my dignity died. But I still turned up. I still sat there. I still watched, and I still learned what I could, even from that distant vantage point. I sat on that stool and tried to muster as much self-respect as I could as I watched everything that went on. In the end, I took in enough to pass the end-of-term test despite having done none of the work. And, unlike Dereck Cruikshank, I still owned both of my eyebrows.

I didn't succeed to spite my physics teacher. I had access to a much bigger stimulus than that. What kept me turning up to school? The receptionist who silently slid Tracker bars to me when I arrived late and hungry, having not eaten since the last free school meal. The PE department arranging matches and track meets that allowed me to be part of a team and excel. The art teacher hell bent on unlocking my creativity and celebrating my progress. And I succeeded because there was one adult who I spent time with every day, who cared about me and who believed in me. Mr Simpson.

With unfailing consistency, he was there for me, letting me know that he not only wanted me to succeed but that he expected me to. It was an expectation that was beginning to rub off on me. Day after day, he helped me build on the resilience that I had inside me to use it as a resource to move me forward. As with Mrs Cook and Mr Williams, his influence was so great that it had an impact on me when he wasn't even in the room.

To be honest, I don't remember much about the content of Mr Simpson's geography lessons (despite how much he banged on about rivers). No child leaves school, bumps into a teacher and says, 'Cor, it wasn't half great in your class. I loved all the data collection you did!' They do, however, remember bizarre stuff related to how the teacher made them feel.

One lesson I remember was an activity that had something to do with getting a herd of bison across the United States. We were split into teams, with me landing on a table of kids who didn't like me – the feeling was very mutual. Mr Simpson listed the roles that needed to be allocated (with one less role than there were team members), and my team got busy deciding who was going to be who. He then called me over to talk to me about something that had nothing to do with the task, and when I returned to my group, all of the roles had been bagged, leaving me with no job. He then announced that the person in the group without a role would be the leader, and they would have the final say on the strategy for the entire trip!

I went to see him after the lesson to explain that I didn't know how to be a leader and that no one in my group would actually listen to me. He told me I had everything I needed because I was great at processing information quickly, and I had a history of making great decisions. I was bamboozled by his confidence in me but fortified by his belief, I connected with my group and somehow led our bison across the United States in first place!

Mr Simpson never veered from his agenda of teaching geography, but along the way he seized every opportunity to engage with his learners and meet their needs. I needed acceptance, validation and friends, and by showing my peers that he respected me, Mr Simpson brought about an unspoken truth that allowed his geography lessons to be a safe space to collaborate and learn.

Human lie detector

As time went on, trying to keep school separate from what was going on at home became increasingly demanding. School was a welcome break, but it was difficult to navigate the day if a teacher who I didn't have a relationship with took the class. They would expect automatic and absolute buy-in from me, which was a huge ask, especially on the days when all I wanted was a warm radiator to sit next to and some hot food.

Many of the regular teachers I had were wonderful human beings who prioritised relationships and engaged us with empathy, but in the gaps I would revert to my belief that this was a temporary pass, and later in the afternoon this bubble would burst. Successfully staying regulated throughout a school day was akin to appearing on a physically exhausting and unwinnable Japanese game show like *Takeshi's Castle*. Even if you did make it past the maze where some doors you ran at were paper and some were not, or the rope bridge with missiles being fired at you, you were unlikely to survive the final challenge of driving your jeep to safety without one of the dragons piercing your tracing paper shield with their water cannons!

Completing the school day often left me inexplicably exhausted, especially so after lunch when I was on a countdown to home time. Mondays were a particular challenge after two days away from the only place where I was able to pretend I was just a regular child and not a prisoner on day release. Weekends at home felt like punishment for a crime I didn't know how to stop committing.

On the days when I struggled, all I really needed was a safe space – the high school equivalent of Mrs Cook's book corner where I could reset and have a chance of coming back down from whatever I'd flipped out about in the first place. It could be something as simple as a request from a teacher, which sounded a little sharp and would put me on alert and in defence mode.

> **Teacher (*in a slightly annoyed expression and tone and without saying 'please'*): 'Pick that coat up.'**
>
> **Me (*feeling unfairly treated by the request*): 'It's not mine.'**
>
> **Teacher (*spoken more harshly and with a little bit of an ego, which feels to me like an adult trying to assert their power over me and triggers the same emotion as when I'm bullied by my stepfather*): 'I didn't ask you whose it was.'**
>
> **Me: (*either kisses teeth, responds aggressively, runs out of the classroom or all three*) ...**

It was around this time that I became convinced I was psychic! I had an uncanny knack for being able to tell when the words and actions of adults were out of alignment with what they actually thought and felt. I scanned adults in school for signs of deceit. My radar was hypersensitive – it had to be. It was the only defence I had for keeping myself safe outside of school. It turned out that I wasn't psychic – I was hypervigilant and good at reading body language along with facial and micro-expressions. It's a skill that those living in some form of chaos learn. You develop an ability to read facial expressions as they provide information about intent and mood, so you can be prepared if something bad is about to happen. While lacking in many tangible ways, the children who need authenticity the most are experts when it comes to sniffing it out.

My everyday home life was an excellent training ground. The majority of my waking hours were spent on constant alert, deciphering body language, facial expressions and moods. I spent my spare time praying to my grandad's God for a rescue (which was either my real dad turning up and being the opposite of what I knew a dad to be or, even better, one of my fabulous teachers taking me home with them), escape (literally running away with the circus – which is why I taught myself to juggle) or dying (always my third and final option but it meant abandoning my brothers so it was something I could only fantasize about).

I watched my stepfather a lot, which was dangerous in itself because catching his eye meant drawing his attention. At first, when he noticed me, I'd adopt a subservient posture, adjusting my body language and facial expression to avoid aggravating him. I genuinely believed that it was something I said or did that made him fly off into a rage. Once I realised that being passive didn't stop him from hurting me, I would set my face to what I thought was an aggressive expression in an attempt to stop him from speaking to me. That didn't work either, but it felt better to stand up for myself and be beaten than accept it without challenge.

Later, in high school, I used the same technique on teachers to prevent them from hurting me – the default behaviour I expected from adults. It was often mistaken for threatening behaviour. One teacher in particular responded by reprimanding me in class for my 'bad attitude', telling me that I 'lacked the character needed for success'. I was angry that he'd made a judgement based on what he saw on the surface. But, most of all, he and I were in agreement about the truth about me. I deserved the detention, but what he saw as punishment was another of those thirty-minute periods of safety and calm in the only place where I felt safe.

No, I'm Paul

By the time Paul started at my high school, I had been in several different foster placements with and without my younger brothers. After fleeing Jason the Pimp, I'd stayed with my nan on and off and had not returned home where my brothers and sister lived with my parents. I hadn't seen Paul for years, and I was excited to see him again. I waited for him at the bus stop on the first day, hiding behind a bush in case my biological mother showed up with him. Unsurprisingly, he was alone, and I rushed over for our big reunion.

He was a shadow of the boy I had left. He had grown a little but was still the smallest eleven-year-old getting off the bus. He was thin and gaunt, had dark rings around his eyes and was generally dirty. He looked nervous and distracted, and when I asked him how things were at home, he mumbled and went quiet. I was worried. What if his teachers didn't see past his scowl? Especially when they found out he was my brother – not exactly a great reputation to live up to.

Focusing on studying seemed pointless and selfish when I should have been protecting my siblings. Paul wouldn't or couldn't talk to me. When I cornered him to talk, his face looked permanently pained, and his eyes seemed to accuse me of abandoning him. I had protected him, stood in the way of our raging stepfather, stole food for him to eat and been a source of income when my stepfather loaned me to his mates. With me gone, Paul became my replacement. In the quad one lunchtime, I started to head over to him when I heard someone ask if he was my brother? He replied, 'No, I'm Paul.' He was a broken boy and it was all my fault.

I had to fix it. I had experienced two years of relative peace at my nan's with an army of social workers and foster parents. What to do next? I had already tried involving adults, but to no avail, so it was now down to me. I'm not sure how I arrived at the decision to pay a visit to my parents' house, but I promised Paul I would be coming round that night. I went back to my nan's to get changed out of my school uniform. It seems like a pointless strategy now, but I wanted my stepfather to think I was grown up so that he wouldn't treat me like he did when I was a child. I felt sick on the bus journey and then walked down the familiar depressing streets with their rubbish-strewn back alleys to the house as if I were on my way to the electric chair. I braced myself before knocking on the door – once I entered that house, I'd have nowhere to run to if it all kicked off.

My parents were out, and I found Paul living in even worse squalor than when I had been there. The house was more disgusting than I remembered. There was a stench of dampness, and it was dirtier than ever, with uncleared mice droppings around the skirting boards. The two younger boys were in an even worse state than Paul and were fighting over a biscuit. The new baby girl was now two years old and sat in a soiled nappy with eyes red raw from crying. Paul sat on the sofa staring at the TV but not in a relaxed, slouched position, on the edge of the seat as if waiting to run. Guilt compounded into hate for myself. This was the impact of me leaving them, not being there to clean up and take care of the kids. It felt like I'd been simultaneously punched in the face and stomach.

I went into human-doing mode and busied myself by trying to introduce some care and nurture. I read stories, cleaned the house as much as I could and laid clothes out for my younger brothers and sister for the next day. There was no iron so I couldn't do much with the school uniform I found scrunched up at the bottom of Paul's bed, which consisted of two blankets on a non-carpeted floor.

By the time my parents arrived back from the pub, it was late and I was in danger of missing the last bus back to my nan's house. They walked in drunk to see me for the first time in three years. My biological mother barely registered me, and my stepfather threw a casual 'Oh yer back, are ya?' in my direction. I was surprised at how well I could suppress my fear and play the part of a gobby teenager. I informed my stepfather that I was there to babysit, and they weren't allowed to leave the kids on their own – something I knew they had been told repeatedly by social services. I told him it was illegal and that I would tell the police if they did it again.

And so it continued. I was reinstated as 'house girl' for my parents, this time looking after three brothers and a sister. My two youngest brothers didn't remember me at first and my sister didn't know me at all, but I won them over by bringing them sweets and paper for them to draw on. My parents still used the tactic of withholding food as a punishment, so all four of them were malnourished. I smuggled food from my nan's house, brushed the knots out of their hair and bought a tube of toothpaste. Although I couldn't afford toothbrushes so I taught them how to use their fingers to sort of brush their teeth. I snuck blankets from my nan's hope chest for their beds. I sat with them at night, singing songs until they fell asleep. They were terrified to go to their rooms alone and told me horrifying stories of the ways my stepfather punished them.

Paul still sat on the edge of his seat, arms folded and knees tightly together and staring straight ahead at nothing in particular. He was withdrawn and barely spoke to me. I knew that he was angry with me for leaving him, and I didn't blame him. He stayed up late and always looked exhausted, just like I must have done when I was physically and emotionally responsible for all the younger ones. I could tell he was glad I was back but still annoyed with me for leaving. In the same way that I didn't trust the adults in my life, he didn't trust me either.

As it approached 11.30pm, we'd prop the door to the stairs open and listen out for the key being drunkenly fumbled in the lock so Paul could dart upstairs and pretend to be asleep. The last few minutes in the house, between my parents arriving and me leaving, were the most dangerous. Both of them were smashed, and my stepfather often tried to grab me as I ran past him and down the road into the dark to get the bus back to my nan's.

I started spending my weekends and school holidays in my parent's house. If I didn't have the money for the bus, I walked there and got the children out of the house as much as I could, feeling that fresh air would somehow make them stronger. Every time I left them the little ones cried, while Paul scowled and retreated back into himself.

Biologists know best

The strain of life at home started to show up in school. It was around that time that Mr Simpson arranged for me to have some one-to-one counselling with a new biology teacher with a huge scar on her face. I liked the fact that she was different and thought that maybe she would understand how it felt to be an outsider.

I was called out of history on Wednesday afternoons. I don't know who was more ecstatic about that – me or Mr R, my long-suffering history teacher. We sat in a small room off the library and talked. Mrs E never mentioned how she had navigated people noticing the scar, and I never dared ask, but we did talk about what we liked and didn't like. I opened up a little about myself, and she gave me the good listening to I desperately needed. For an entire hour! Every Wednesday! It was bliss.

After a few weeks, she seemed to smile less and became slightly more impatient. I clammed up when she told me we only had a few sessions left. Up until then there had been no conditions, and it had felt to me like a real relationship. I read the change in mood and deduced that she was being paid to care, which wasn't the same as genuinely caring.

She asked me what was worrying me, and I told her that I was afraid my nan would die on account of her being really old, and then I would be back in foster care. She asked me how old my nan was, and when I said fifty-five, she looked insulted, scoffed and told me that wasn't old at all.[7]

In the penultimate session, she reminded me that it was my last chance to tell her about anything that was making my life difficult. Despite feeling pressured and rushed and unsure about what would happen next, I wanted to tell her I was scared. That I had nightmares about when my stepfather would come into my bedroom at night and do unspeakable things to my body. I thought that maybe if she knew, I would be able to have another set of sessions with her and enjoy the luxury of being listened to some more. In a quiet voice, I articulated something I'd managed to tell two other adults before her – my stepfather had forced me to have sex with him.

Her expression became stern. Was she cross with me? I begged her not to tell anyone and made her promise. She said to leave it with her, and that she would get back to me. I then spent an entire week waiting. Every moment was agonising. I had just shared my deepest, darkest secret with her, and now she was walking around with my vulnerability in her hands – for a whole week. I looked out for her around the school but didn't see her. What if she didn't come back? What if she told another teacher at school? What if my stepfather found out and finally kept his promise to kill me?

Today, there is a legal obligation to report any and all disclosures. Keeping children safe is everyone's responsibility. We need more education and conversation about child neglect and abuse *prevention* rather than waiting until it happens and reacting appropriately.

Successful safeguarding is reliant on the critical human element of a person ready and willing to listen. This was the third time I'd tried to tell an adult what my stepfather was doing to me. The first was a social worker returning my brother and me home from a foster care placement. I interrupted him singing to 'More Than a Woman' by the Bee Gees and blurted out that my stepfather came into my room at night and hurt me. He paused, staring straight ahead, said nothing and drove me back to my parent's house.

The second time, I bunked off school to report my parents to the social services. The receptionist tried to put me off by telling me that they were very busy, but I told her I'd wait, and wait I did. Eventually, a man with a clipboard came and

---

7   Now I'm an adult, I realise that 55 isn't in the slightest bit old at all and still feel bad about the unintentional insult! I totally understand she wasn't able to hide her offence!

took me into a room. The disbelief in his questioning still echoes in my head today:

'Why haven't you mentioned this before?'

'Are you just making this up to get attention?'

Each time, I could only manage a weak 'I don't know' while shame and despair choked my real answers. A few years later, I was allowed to see the files that social services had kept on me as a child. Among them, I found a sheet of A4 paper covered with scrawled notes that recorded that very meeting:

> Half-caste stepdaughter.
>
> Vivid imagination.
>
> Tells lies.
>
> Stepfather less likely to hurt his own biological (white) children.

This third disclosure saw me face a week of nerve-jangling panic lasting until the following Wednesday. She began our session by chatting about how I could try to control my anger and asked me if I understood what consequences were. What a stupid question! Of course, I did – I was a living consequence. Then, as the session drew to a close, she told me how nice it had been getting to know me. In desperation, I mumbled, 'What about what I told you last week? About my stepfather?' It stung having to refer to the abuse, but I couldn't leave without knowing what was going to happen next. What had she done with my horrible secret?

'It's best you forget about that and not mention it again,' she replied.

My first thought was disappointment. It was evident to me that she had discussed what I told her in confidence with someone else. Who? It must be someone from school, another teacher who knew me. She didn't know what to do, she asked for advice and someone must have told her that I couldn't be trusted, was probably lying and that she should advise me to forget about it.

I wanted to tell her that she'd let me down in more ways than I could count, but she was smiling at me and ushering me out of the door. With every step I took, I became more engulfed in rage and helplessness. As I left, I looked her in the eye and told her that her face was disgusting. It was a futile and childish attack, designed to hurt her like she'd hurt me by pretending to care.

A botched kidnap

When I wasn't at school, I was at my parents' house with my brothers and sister, running it like a Caramel Taupe[8] Mary Poppins. I developed various distraction strategies: songs, games, origami and juggling, all in an attempt to divert from the sense of danger.

One evening I arrived late to find my stepfather had tied the door handles shut, trapping my youngest brothers in their bedrooms. An old trick he'd used on me in the cellar. I used a calming voice to get through to them both and cheerily sang songs while sawing through the rope with a kitchen knife. I disassociated, trying to block out the trauma of watching my brothers go through what I had. I was all out of hope, having resigned myself to the fact that no adult was coming to save them.

Protecting my siblings became a wedge between me and the Category 1 adults at school. They didn't know, I didn't tell them, but I still felt betrayed and furious. I silently blamed them. So I made a plan: pass their stupid tests, finish school, get a job and buy a house big enough for me, Paul and our siblings. That mission may have been unrealistic but it gave a thirteen-year-old me who didn't yet have a firm grasp of compound interest a glimmer of hope.

As I spent more time with my siblings, school became a side quest. I tried to train Paul in escape plans. Like a drill sergeant, I made him practice locking the bathroom, climbing out the window and scaling the kitchen roof down into the alley. My younger siblings watched from the backyard, shouting encouragement and cheering him on.

At night, after bedtime, Paul would sit in silence. I'd pressure him to be strong for the others, but I allowed my desperation and exasperation to come through and only made him withdraw more. With each visit, I'd find new bruises and wounds caused by our stepfather's belt. With no first aid, I used my socks to cover cuts and taught them to hold bleeding limbs above their hearts – a trick I picked up from a first aid book I read during a time I was holed up in the library. Bedwetting was a constant battle. With no sheets to change, I flipped mattresses over and over trying to find the least stained side to lay an unsoiled

---

8   I began using 'Caramel Taupe' as a silent protest. I was fed up with forms that had no box for me to tick. 'White, Black, Asian, Other (Please specify)' annoyed me for its lack of adherence to alphabetical order and the fact that I didn't enjoy being described as 'Other'. After a bit of research at a DIY store I found a compromise I was happy with. I'd tick 'Other' and on the line next to 'Please specify' I would write: 'Caramel Taupe' (according to the paint chart in B&Q) which I considered to be specific enough.

blanket on. I was doing the best I could for them, and that was about as effective as bailing a sinking ship with a teaspoon.

I knew the only way for them to be safe and away from danger was for them to be placed with a foster family. I managed to get Paul out by coaxing him to my nan's 'for a visit'. My nan took one look at the state of him and made her mind up there and then. He never went back. I was afraid of returning to their house without him but my parents barely noticed. My stepfather muttered that Paul wasn't 'one of his own', and my biological mother said nothing at all. I guess social services were involved, but I wasn't aware. Paul was safe. Now I just needed a plan for the rest.

Even during these dark times, I had the memory of a handful of adults that had believed me and stood for me – Mrs Cook, Mr Williams. I failed to find the courage to trust someone. I believed I deserved what I'd lived through and couldn't risk losing Mr Simpson as my only advocate by revealing the truth.

The late nights were tiring, and I arrived late for school most days. Detentions became the pain in the backside they were designed to be. Every minute I had to sit and be sorry left my siblings waiting longer for hugs and food.

The kids asked where Paul was and I whispered promises: one day we'd all live together in a big house. My nan had no more space and things were getting desperate. The situation got worse. One brother smuggled matches, hoping to start a fire so the fire brigade would come. My sister pulled buttons from her clothes and swallowed them, in the hope that an ambulance would take her away to safety ...

There was only one thing left to do. Kidnap them.

I planned to take the kids to my nan's as soon as my parents left for the pub, but fear stopped me from taking action. Before I knew it, I'd waited too long and heard the key turn in the lock. Standing my ground, I told my drunk parents the kids weren't staying another night. My stepfather lunged, slammed me against the wall, pinning me by the throat. My biological mother screamed at him not to let me take them. In the back room, my friend, who I had taken along for support, and siblings watched in horror.

Seeing the kids out of bed sent my stepfather into a rage. Dropping me to the ground, he went after the little ones, grabbing at them and flinging them against the door to the stairs. Unable to stand by and watch, I launched myself onto his back and screamed for my friend to take the kids and run.

I hated myself for touching him but had to make him stop, no matter what the cost. Within seconds, he'd thrown me onto the sofa and began violently punching me in the face and stomach. I curled up, hoping the screams would bring help. Running out of physical steam, he paused to shout familiar insults, calling me a 'little b*tch', a 'black b*stard' and a 'useless n*gger who should have been drowned at birth'. I could have run when he stormed off to the kitchen, before he came back with the knife.

Pinning me down with the weight of his body he pressed the knife to my throat and whispered horrors into my ear. The alcohol and cigarette smell so close to my face triggered deeper terror, and I wet myself. He laughed. I cried. Sensing his victory, he released his grip, and I bolted, once again leaving my siblings in danger and knowing I'd made things arguably worse. He chased me to the front door, screaming not to come back until I'd stopped 'crying like a girl'.

My friend and I made the bus journey home in silence. I didn't have the capacity to worry about her emotional state. I sat broken and bruised, feeling defeated and smelling of urine, squeezing the hand of my trembling friend and making her swear on her own life that she would tell no one at school about what she had seen.

You'll never amount to anything

I went through the motions at school. Time passed, and exams approached. Mr Simpson had been asking me what I planned to do after school. I'd given up on the foolish notion of getting a job and buying a house for my siblings to escape to. I had no plans for the next day, let alone the future. All I could think of was to continue on into sixth form. I couldn't cope with any more change. He advised me to follow my passions, but I didn't know what they were, or even if I had any. Everything I wanted was so out of reach – for my siblings to be rescued, to feel free from the crushing dark thoughts I lived with. I mentioned that I was good at looking after children so perhaps I could do a childcare course. He replied, 'Yes, and then get your degree and become a teacher.' I had no idea what a degree was and was too preoccupied to find out. I told him I just wanted to stay at school, and I'm sure he must have pulled some strings to get me into my school sixth form with my less-than-perfect grades.

From day one, I was behind. My body made it to school and sat in the library, but my mind was on the safety of my siblings. I struggled to focus to care about my studies. Homework piled up and I stopped eating. The pressure of letting down the one adult who believed in me became too much.

When I told Mr Simpson I was dropping out, he didn't express disappointment. Instead: 'You've outgrown us. Let's get you a place at college for September.' The guy never failed to amaze me! He wasn't furious, and he didn't tell me I'd let myself down or that I was a waste of space. He put his own agenda and feelings to one side and reframed my own truth. The truth that I mattered, that I was important, that I was more than just a victim of circumstances. He took my failure and fashioned it into a brighter and more hopeful future. That's what Everyday Hero educators do. They don't just teach, it goes much further than that. Mr Simpson held up a mirror to the version of me that there was no way I could see alone.

Thanks to Mr Simpson I now had a plan, and he delivered the set of application forms to me before I could change my mind – reminding me of my promise to carry on with my education. He always called it 'my education' like it belonged to me. He viewed the school as lucky to have me, unlike Mrs K, a member of the senior leadership team who'd had more than her fair share of my outbursts over the last few years.

With my application for a deferred college place submitted, I had to visit Mrs K to tell her my decision. To say she wasn't happy with me now I was giving up would be an understatement. She informed me that leaving school was tantamount to throwing my life away and that I lacked the consistency of effort to start college the following September. My final memory of high school was her telling me that I should be more grateful for the chances I had been given and that if I walked away now I would 'never amount to anything'.

I did what any self-respecting teenager would do in that situation. I pulled myself up to my full height, smiled sarcastically and swaggered off, shouting over my shoulder that I was going to get a degree and come back and show her, so she could shove it where 'the sun don't shine'. Not my finest hour but someone had to be the adult, right?

Years later, at a theme park near Hull in the North of England, Mr Simpson and I stand at the back of the audience beside the face-painting hut as the show (minus one clown) goes on. He introduces me to his family. His wife smiles in a way that suggests this is not the first time someone has approached her husband, starting a sentence with the three most powerful words a teacher can hear from a former student …

'Because of you.'

My words garble out as I explain that being a clown is my summer job. That I made it to university. That I was training to be a teacher, just like him – only minus the slight obsession with how oxbow lakes are formed.

As I struggle breathlessly to find the words to describe the full circle moment I felt, Mr Simpson watches, listens and nods with a soft smile.

'That's good,' he says. 'You're still on track. Keep going.'

Mr Simpson's Legacy

High school was another adverse childhood experience for me.

Navigating unwritten rules, hiding behind a carefully constructed front, trying to contain the fury I felt towards adults and swallowing the shame of what I was going home to every night was exhausting. I alternated between the hyperfocus I needed to actually make it into the building and the complete overwhelm caused by staying for a full day. I lived the raw reality of being invisible in plain sight.

Mr Simpson is the reason that didn't define me.

If primary school was a place of sanctuary, high school felt like an impossible race up a five-year staircase. Some students set off in Nike trainers with years of trial runs behind them, but I was still sat in the changing rooms, panicking about being found out whilst trying to fashion suitable running footwear out of abandoned plastic bags.

Mr Simpson was less concerned with comparing my milestones to those of others who'd started closer to the finish line, or with those with even fewer resources than me who hadn't made it to the starting block. He encouraged me to focus on my smallest next step and marked every small climb as if it was worthy of an Olympic medal.

While others saw a *vulnerable* and *disadvantaged* student displaying *challenging behaviour* – someone who was persistently late, difficult to engage and didn't appear to care – he saw a *valuable* young person from an *under-resourced area* displaying *distressed behaviour* and brimming with potential and possibility. Some were distracted by my rollercoaster ride of silence to screaming, but Mr Simpson focused on the child behind the front and translated school into drinkable water – a lifeline in the turbulent salt-ridden ocean I was swimming/drowning in.

There were no grand gestures in his playbook. His superpower was boring textbook consistency! He showed up. He checked in. He stood. Like one of those guys on the Waltzers at a fair who stand cool, balanced and unaffected while you're being spun around and trying not to throw up.

Mr Simpson stood. In spite of the pressure he was under to hit targets and (presumably) to assert geography as the undisputed heavyweight champion of the curriculum, he took the time to greet me, to offer a connection. He assumed the best of me and showed me unconditional positive regard. Every. Single. Day.

I wish I could say my experience belonged to another era. That the system had evolved beyond recognition. That all young people were met exactly where they are, no matter their starting point. That off-rolling wasn't a thing. I wish isolation booths weren't still used in place of restorative support. I wish the school-to-prison pipeline was fiction. I wish safeguarding never failed. I wish unconscious bias wasn't still quietly writing kids out of their own stories.

But the truth is, the adults in schools are exclusively human.

After thirty years working in and with those in this sector, I can say with my hand on my heart that there are overwhelmingly more adults in school standing, giving of themselves, making sacrifices, fighting for the highest good of kids, and even risking their own mental and physical health to the point of burnout in order to show up for students. If you're wondering how some schools manage to keep going even when they're overwhelmed and underfunded, look to the staff.

And still, our system today can make it incredibly hard to keep standing.

The *Timpson Review of School Exclusion* laid bare what many already knew. Almost 80% of children who end up permanantly excluded from school are already facing the greatest challenges – poverty, social care involvement, or additional learning needs. 11% are juggling all three. Add on being a Black or brown boy and the odds are stacked even higher.[9]

It raises the question of what kind of a system puts pressure on schools to deliver identical results regardless of the starting point of the students and then penalises leaders for prioritising people over performance metrics that fail to include the complete picture? It takes a brave leader to stand in the face of the ever-mounting pressure on schools and say 'We're going to do what's best for the children – no matter what it costs us' when it could actually cost them a low Ofsted rating, a dip in staff retention, a reduction in funding, an increase in mental and physical health issues and even their own job.

One leader summed it up perfectly: 'We're probably at the bottom of every league table going, but we're winning at showing up and serving the community we are in.'

The Timpson Review stated that 'it cannot be the job of schools alone to take action to understand and address the complex underlying needs that children may have'.[10] In cases where the community works together, especially when schools are working closely with their Virtual School, accessing all of the resources and support available from these particular Everyday Heroes, positive disruption happens.[11] It all starts with one person wanting change.

People ask me how to be more like my five Everyday Hero teachers.

If you're asking that, you probably already are.

Mr Simpson wasn't a saviour, opting for value over rescue as his weapon of choice.[12] He was just consistently himself and consistently my champion. It took me five years to grasp that he was truly in my corner. That's the payoff of not giving up. Mr Simpson never tried to be my family or fill the void at home.

Instead, he showed me that when family fails, community can become everything.

---

9 E. Timpson, *Timpson Review of School Exclusion* (London: Department for Education, 2019). Available at: https://assets.publishing.service.gov.uk/government/uploads/system/uploads/attachment_data/file/807862/Timpson_review.pdf, p. 10.

10 Timpson, *Timpson Review*, p. 6.

11 If you're working in a school, do yourself a favour and make friends with your Virtual School. NAVSH is the National Association of Virtual School Heads. It's honestly one of the most powerful and positive forces to be made statutory in education in the last decade. Every single Virtual School I've worked with has shown me what heart-led leadership looks like in action – compassion, courage and a relentless refusal to give up on the children who need us most. I'm such a proud NAVSH fangirl that I've created a series of exclusive videos for them, called Bitesize Jaz. These short, high-impact clips are packed with inspiration and are completely free for every school. Reach out to your Virtual School and get access today.

12 S. Blandford, *Born To Fail? Social Mobility, A Working Class View* (Woodbridge: John Catt Educational, 2017).

In today's high-pressure education system, it's easy to forget the most powerful thing you can do for a child is simply to show up. The same way. Every day. Without fanfare. Without judgement. With belief. That's what Mr Simpson did.

That consistency protected the fragile, paper-thin skin slowly forming over my deep, open wounds. It taught me what true safety felt like. I did go to college – just like I promised him I would. Then university. Then into education. I became a teacher, a coach, a consultant and an international government advisor. Then, as a result of being consistently 10% braver myself, I gave a TEDx Talk[13] which was the catalyst for an international speaking career and ultimately me sitting down and writing this book to remind you how much of an Everyday Hero you truly are!

For the five tumultuous years that I navigated unprocessed trauma, Mr Simpson was Savlon in human form – Human Savlon! And yet he never knew. I never told him what a difference he made to me. Most of our 'conversations' entailed long periods of me silently staring at the ground while he talked me up while leaning on the nearest wall, with his sleeves rolled up.

On behalf of the young human you're already being Mr Simpson for, but who doesn't yet have the emotional literacy to express what this means to them ...

Thank you.

The chairs were definitely smaller but the smell was unmistakably familiar.

I stood behind the last desk on the back row next to the window in my old high school form room. I'd been invited back to deliver the closing keynote at a conference in the very place I'd run screaming from thirty years earlier.

Though the building had been considerably extended and modernised, the main entrance and late corridor remained unchanged. As I slowly retraced my steps down the late corridor, recreating the same path I'd taken many times on my daily walk of shame, I'd be lying if I said it wasn't triggering. My brain glitched between the wounded student survivor I was and the woman I've become: mother, international speaker, resilience ninja – still healing but no longer hiding.

---

13 See http://bit.ly/JazTED. It's a 10-minute assertion of your Everyday Hero status. Watch it and share it with someone who needs a reminder of how much difference they make.

I'd been invited by Ian Gilbert of Independent Thinking and I'm forever grateful for him expertly helping me to navigate that day as my mind alternated between the past and the present, between hopelessness and agency.[14]

In that form room I had arrived late to hundreds of registrations. I spent just as many afternoon dismissals clutching the legs of the chair I'd placed on top of the desk so that the cleaners could hoover underneath. Closing my eyes I could see Mr Simpson perched on the edge of his desk, calm, unshakeable and consistently asserting his belief in me. Where was he now? How old would he be? Was it too late to thank him?

Later, I entered the huge hall where the staff of the entire trust were making their way to their seats. A young woman moved against the flow of people straight towards me. She had a familiar look about her and her energy and smile suggested we had met before.

It transpired that we had.

We'd met when she was five years old, watching a clown show with her dad, at a theme park.

Time folded in on itself as Mr Simpson's daughter and I hugged – crying, talking, clutching hands, all at once. Through tears of healing, release and bone-deep gratitude, I tried to explain how her dad had been my high school lifeline. That he had been the wall between making it through and something much darker.

She nodded, already knowing, and confirmed he'd been that for me and so many others before and since. I was one ripple of his impact, she was another, now teaching in the same school,.

One teacher's quiet consistency creating ripples that transform generations.

Not something you can easily capture with a spreadsheet or a set of exam results. It goes much further than that to hearts rekindled, spirits restored and lives transformed.

---

14 See https://www.independentthinking.co.uk/.

Be Mr Simpson: Reflections

1. **Bridge the belonging gulf**

   Without a doubt, my most difficult transition took place during the Summer of No Belonging. You know, when you don't belong to primary school anymore but don't belong to secondary school yet either. Those long weeks are hard when school is your home. How can you improve transitions in your setting? At the beginning and end of the school day, in and out of the weekend and mid or end of term breaks?

2. **Indulge in a spot of positive disruption**

   Various derivatives of the word *disrupt* made regular appearances on my school reports over the years. Mr Simpson showed me that I could turn my superpower into something more powerful by inserting the word *positive* in front of it. Positive disruption interrupts limiting narratives. Try it the next time you find yourself in an argument and note how quickly it dissolves tension.

3. **Flip your Bs**

   Get your Bs in the right order. In primary school, I was told: you *belong* here, we *believe* in you, and guess what happens when B1 and B2 are strong – your *behaviour* changes. In high school, the Bs were reversed. If you *behave* in the way we deem acceptable and *believe* in the delayed gratification that education delivers, then you can *belong*. In that case, it's easier to find belonging by joining a gang. Mr Simpson asserted belonging as a non-negotiable. What order are your Bs in? (Clue: for an accurate and unfiltered answer, ask your students.)

4. **Rip up your behaviour policy**

   Interested in a zero cost and neutral way of improving your school's behaviour policy? Print it out, rip up the title page, print out another page that reads 'Relationship Policy' and stick it on the front. Et voilà! A 'Behaviour Policy' gives 'Here is how we want you to behave and here's a comprehensive breakdown of the 300 different ways we will punish you when you don't!' Whereas a 'Relationship Policy' is 'Here's how we're going to show up for you to support and encourage you to grow into the best you can be and in return here's what we'd like from you.' Which one would you prefer to be on the other side of?

5. **Rebrand resilience**

    Resilience isn't about keeping a stiff upper lip or being a doormat – it's about shortening the time between being on the floor and getting back up again. Just as athletes try to shave time off each marathon, work on reducing your recovery time. Bouncing back used to take me years, then months, weeks, days, hours ... and I'm working on minutes! How are you modelling this agility for your students?

6. **The experts**

    Words build worlds. The language we use about children shapes the way we see them, teach them and treat them. I get that 'disadvantaged', 'vulnerable' and 'challenging behaviour' are shortcuts for describing children. Having to read my own 'rap sheets' when I was 16 and seeing many of these words used by professionals to describe me had a profound impact. As a teacher, I decided not to use any words to describe a child that I wouldn't be prepared to print on a T-shirt and have them wear. Labels stick and aren't helpful when you're in the business of 're-storying'[15] lives. I've asked school leaders what they call children who *aren't* disadvantaged and heard, without irony, 'We call them the non-disadvantaged' or worse, 'We just call them the normal ones.' Imagine being on the other side of that language. What subtle shifts in your vocabulary could change the story you're telling – and the story you're living?

7. **Ask the experts**

    Speaking in a large London secondary school, I asked a hall full of Year 11s to raise their hand if they felt the staff in their school were *genuinely* for them. A few hands crept up ... but what filled the hall louder than any word was the collective *huff* displaying the disbelief that hung heavy in the air. I followed up with, 'How many of you feel that *one or two* teachers in this school are for you?' Every single hand went up. It made me wonder who those adults were and whether they were all thinking of the same teachers. What would the reaction from the students in your school be?

8. **Be Human Savlon**

    When students push you away, it's rarely personal and more often protection. It's incredibly unlikely that the student has been lying awake at night thinking of ways to annoy you the next day! Trauma doesn't trust easily and healing doesn't come from a single heroic act. It is kickstarted and continued

---

15 Okay, I may have made this word up, but it works, no? Also, it's the title of the film based on my second book, so no pinching it!

by your quiet, consistent presence. What do you need to invest in yourself to be the human who shows up, again and again, after being pushed away by a child in pain? And who in your life needs you to show up for them today?

9. **Rewrite the unwritten rules**

    I'm talking about those unspoken, quiet expectations that shape who belongs, who thrives and who gets left behind. If you're a leader, ask your team to anonymously write down the unspoken rules of your workplace. If you work with young people, ask them what rules nobody ever told them, but everyone seems to follow. Then take a breath – because what you hear might be eye-opening, uncomfortable ... and exactly what you need.

10. **Focus behind the front**

    If you want to measure your legacy, don't stop at phonics scores or GCSE results. Look at who your students become at 35. That's where the real data lives – in the kind of humans they grow into, in the choices they make when no one's watching, in the way they encourage their own children. The system measures outcomes. You change lives. Never let the day-to-day busy-ness convince you otherwise.

Miss Archer
The One Who Taught Me Audacity

I'd like to say my plan to get into university was meticulously crafted. It wasn't. Instead, it was cobbled together from three unlikely ingredients: raw desperation, borrowed audacity and quite possibly the worst Scottish accent ever attempted.

It started with my A level grades: two spectacularly solid Es.[1] To me, just completing the course and sitting the exams felt like successfully climbing Everest. To university admissions departments, it was more like turning up at Base Camp in your vest, pants and a pair of flip-flops.

The end of full-time education coincided with the end of my time living in the place I loosely referred to as home. That put a lot of emphasis on securing a place at university. Failing wasn't just about not reaching my goal. Continuing on to university meant proving those teachers who had believed in me right and fulfilling my dream, with the added bonus of a place to live in the form of student accommodation. With no plan B or family to fall back on, I'd placed all of my eggs into one poorly constructed basket.

Standing in the college foyer, I gripped the manila envelope in my hand. I already knew that my results would not be good enough to secure my conditional university offer before I'd torn it open. Not really knowing why, I headed to the trio of sofas in the theatre that was Miss Archer's office and my tutor's room. Miss Archer stood wearing her familiar corduroys with back pockets on the front, so it looked like they were the wrong way round. She probably already knew my grades and was waiting for me to turn up. The thought of opening the envelope made a little bit of sick come up in the back of my throat.

'Well?' she asked in her usual straight-to-the-point manner.

Masking shame with anger, I avoided making eye contact and stropped past her, sinking into the middle of the three sofas before starting to well up.

Miss Archer calmly offered me a tissue from the box on her desk. Her kindness made me feel worse. I'd let her down and let myself down. I was a worthless

---

1 I got three A levels but can't find the other certificate. I think it was an N – which I'm pretty sure stands for 'Nearly an A level' so let's go with two-and-a-half A levels!

failure – and I had the certification to prove it! I was angry at myself for daring to believe I could be deserving of my dream, but I directed my anger towards her. Slapping the tissue box to the floor, I tore into her.

Miss Archer stood there, both hands stuffed deep in her pockets, watching me fall apart. I was railing against her, the system and the universe in general for letting me believe I could ever be more than a street kid from the estates. She waited patiently until I ran out of steam, regarding me as if I'd just asked some innocuous question about Stanislavski's impact on 20th-century theatre. Then she delivered the sentence that would change everything:

> **Miss Archer:** 'It's a setback, but if you were truly committed, you'd ring every university in this country until someone gave you a place.'
>
> **Me:** 'What? Well, that would take days!'
>
> **Miss Archer** (*preparing to leave, as if an acceptable compromise had been met*): 'Ahh, good. You've already got a plan.'

Back at the community house, I grabbed the thick, weighty UCAS handbook and untangled the spiral wire that attached the handset to the phone.[2] The only strategy I could come up with was to start at 'A' in the handbook and work my way through.

I ended up chatting to a lovely Scottish lady who asked me about my grades.

'I've got two Es,' I replied.

'Two As?' said the lady in her beautiful sing-song Scottish accent. 'Well done! How aboot you come fur a wee interview?'

Assuming she'd misheard me, I corrected her: 'No, no, not As. *Es*. E for elephant, you know?'

'Oh, two *Es*, I see. In that case, I'm afraid it's a noo.'

That's when it hit me. When I say the <ee> phoneme in my East Midlands accent, it sounds a tiny bit like the <ay> phoneme in a Scottish accent! It dawned on me that this linguistic loophole might just work in my favour. Currently, it appeared that the only thing standing between me and a university place was being born on the wrong side of the Scottish border – a problem with a surprisingly simple solution.

Picking up the phone again, I skipped to the Bs (in case all of the universities beginning with A were mates), called a university in a small town in the middle

---

2   Yes, an actual phone. This was a time in history before everyone had internet enabled devices at their disposal.

of England and prayed that no Scot had emigrated there. Then, in the worst Scottish accent you could imagine:

'Helloo there! Yes, I'd like tae come and join your wee university course. Qualifications? Well, I have two ... ayys.'

The woman on the other end of the phone sounded a bit confused, but, to my complete surprise, it worked! They invited me for an interview. I hung up the phone and immediately entered full-on panic mode.

What have I done?

What exactly was my long-term plan here? Pretend to be Scottish for four years?

What was Miss Archer going to say?

One small step

Miss Archer's form room wasn't so much a classroom as a theatrical junk shop that happened to have students in it. The college theatre auditorium, with its high ceiling and constant smell of floor polish, was home to eclectic collection of props that looked like they'd been rescued from various charity shops over the decades. At one end stood the formal stage with its heavy velvet curtains. At the other, three totally mismatched sofas formed a cosy island in the middle of the chaos.

Those sofas were a sanctuary. All of them were on their last legs. One had a suspicious spring that could catapult you into next week if you sat on it at the wrong angle. Another was covered in a brown velvet that looked old enough to have been liberated from Churchill's War Rooms. The third was a particularly eye-watering floral number with exposed patches of foam that were definitely not fire retardant. They were hideous. They were perfect.

Miss Archer herself was equally distinctive. She had a mass of curly black hair with some silver strands starting to poke through. She spoke in short, matter-of-fact sentences as if words were too expensive and getting to the point was prudent budgeting. But her eyes gave her away – they sparkled with a mix of mischief and fierce intelligence that suggested she could see right through any performance you tried to put on.

My tutor group consisted of quite an eclectic bunch of students who were wonderfully random enough for me not to stand out as the weird one. Miss Archer found space among the piles of props from previous productions for the emotional baggage of every young person who entered the hall. She wasn't mumsy in any way. I loved her consistent forthrightness and unshockability. Nothing surprised her, and you could be forgiven for mistaking her demeanour for someone who wasn't a fan of emotion. It was quite the opposite. Miss Archer knew what was possible and was single-minded in her ability to hold a vision of success for you even before you could hold it yourself.

She was fiercely present with her students. It didn't matter where you were or what state you were in, there was space for it, as long as you were open to winning. With her around – even when she was buried under admin, organising piles of props in shopping trollies or marking papers – her sofas were our home. To me those sofas were reminiscent of the book corner in Mrs Cook's classroom. I knew I was safe there, accepted, acknowledged and valued.

Further education freedom fighter

At almost seventy years old, my nan had agreed to take in my brother and four-year-old sister. There wasn't enough room, resources or food for all three of us, so aged seventeen I moved out. My new home was a community house and offered the kind of independent living that my classmates dreamed about. The reality was less romantic. My student allowance barely covered the rent and left nothing for luxuries like bus fare or hot meals. I walked the four-mile round trip to college, arriving soaked on rainy days to dry myself against radiators during lessons. When the weather turned brutal, I'd splash out on bus fare and skip lunch.

I spent my first year of college feeling numb, kind of shell-shocked from years of being in survival mode. I've since learned that that kind of dissociated state is strongly linked to adverse childhood experiences (ACEs). It's not just *what* happened to you that matters – it's how your brain learned to make sense of it and how those experiences shaped the way you understand yourself and others. If no one helps you to develop those skills before you become an adult, your brain tends to step in to protect you by switching off or disconnecting completely in order for you to continue surviving. It's not that you're broken, just that it's the safest thing to do at the time, which brings us to a bit of a bad news/good news sitch. Bad news – it can leave you with an intense feeling that you don't belong in your own skin. The good news? That wiring isn't fixed. With the right support, you can learn to reconnect, stay present and rewrite the story.

Unfortunately, the cocktail of survivor's guilt and imposter syndrome I was suffering from was debilitating. When you're in pain, you very much would like the pain to stop. When you're being hurt, you look for ways to get away from the source of the hurt. I sought to control the controllables, only there didn't seem to be many.

College represented my last hurdle before university and my goal of being in a position to get all of my siblings to safety. I reasoned that getting a degree would put me on a par with the adults making decisions about our lives, so if I had one too, I'd have to be taken seriously, and they'd have to listen to me. But having a roof over my head and a secure place at college brought a new level of security. The gap left by reducing anxiety was immediately filled with the new challenge of what was probably a form of PTSD, including being overwhelmed by simple tasks like arriving at college with the equipment I needed for the day. I couldn't seem to hold anything in my head – especially where I'd put my keys! At the same time I found myself hyperfocused on other tasks – heightened by the worry of letting people down. The anger I'd used to mask my despair turned to sadness and exhaustion, and I still hadn't finished the uphill marathon.

On good days, I leaned in, relied on my friends for support and fixed my eye on the prize. On bad days, I was a bitter, argumentative teenager, biting back my nan's favourite phrase when classmates chatted about regular college student stuff like buying clothes or getting a lift to college from their parents: 'You don't know you're even born.'

My adult-sized worries were relentless. My nan looking after my teenage brother and four-year-old sister while pulling two cleaning shifts a day and struggling with arthritis. Two of my younger brothers were being repeatedly moved between different foster homes, and my youngest brother – another new baby – still living with my parents, he was in more danger than the judge who'd dismissed my testimony in one of the court cases as 'far-fetched and unbelievable' could comprehend. Even after my stepfather's suspended sentence, the baby remained with him and my biological mother. I was obsessed with the fear of history repeating itself.

I was constantly anxious and drowning in unprocessed trauma. Generally fatigued from having to justify myself (to myself) I started to find ways to punish myself, which felt like a form of relief. I no longer lived with my parents, but they were living in my head rent-free.

Every morning, I left the community house and reached the main road, and I faced the same choice: turn right towards the uphill struggle of education or an easy left back to life on the streets. Turning left offered a seductive escape – no more exhausting attempts to believe in my potential, no more trying to convince others I was acceptable as a human. Instead, it only required submission into blessed numbness. When I couldn't hang on to the positives, two negatives stopped me: I couldn't abandon my siblings, and I was determined not to be anything like my parents. Avoiding that second fate was my biggest driving force. I had momentum. What I lacked was fuel in the tank.

Wrestling with being driven versus being present has been a constant feature throughout my life. While I understand that it's influenced by the misplaced guilt that many of those who have experienced childhood trauma feel, I've been reluctant to tone down my drive because it's the reason I'm still alive today. One of my more wonderful therapists described it as having three circles containing fear, drive and self-compassion. As the fear circle grew, my drive circle grew to combat that, with the result of an amazing ability to continue to overcome adversity. The downside, and it's quite a big one, was that my self-compassion circle had become the size of a beret that a particularly stylish ladybird might favour.

I was weary of being myself. My head was like an internet browser with forty-nine tabs open that I constantly cycled between, seemingly unable to follow a thought or task to the end, from the moment I woke up to the moment I fell asleep. Sleep was hard, my mind whirred like an engine, and I found rest almost impossible. It started to make logical sense to consider ways of not being me. I wasn't afraid of death. It had been a constant parameter while growing up. My grandad was in pain, until he died and then the pain stopped. Simples. My biological mother used to pause when passing the roundabout near the shops to open her coat, show me the kitchen knife she had hidden inside and explain her plan to take me into the middle of the roundabout and 'stab me in the heart'. My stepfather had regularly described exactly how he was going to kill me: 'When I'm done with ya I'm gonna drown ya like a dog in the bath and then bury ya body in the cellar where no one will find ya.'

I fantasized about my brain being switched off, or at least being in suspended animation so that I could pause, rest, breathe. It seemed like a rational response to someone too focused on failures to see how far she'd come. When existence costs that much, the power to end it feels like the only control you have left.

Rational versus suicidal thoughts

During my two years at college, I had three phenomenal female Category 1 tutors in my life: Miss Archer, Miss Jones and Mrs Mountford.

Miss Jones taught typing with a side helping of self-respect. She cast me in a production of the musical *Hair* and refused to accept anyone using the word 'just' when describing themselves. Mrs Mountford had a pastoral role and a cosy office. Miss Archer insisted I go and see Mrs Mountford when she noticed I was displaying signs of withdrawing from life. Mrs Mountford was the one asking the question.

'Have you ever had suicidal thoughts?'

I suspected the 'correct answer' was probably no, but it sounded suspiciously like a double jeopardy, jackpot-losing trick question.

'Having suicidal thoughts' implied, at least to me, a proactive commitment to a course of action. Commitment requires consistent energy, clear thinking and other things I struggled with. I was opting out not opting in. I just wanted the trauma merry-go-round to slow down enough for me to get off.

If she had asked me:

'Do you wish you'd never been born?'

'Do you hate yourself?'

'Do you hide in the bathroom and scratch at your skin until you bleed?'

'Have you repeatedly found yourself leaning precariously over the edge of the bridge above the M1 motorway without being sure of how you got there?'

Any of those questions would have been easy to answer.

'Yeah, of course. Haven't you?'

The slightly sucky side of social mobility

My college had a very clear culture that the vast majority of the adults working there bought into. There was a foundational belief that not everything of value could be measured on a spreadsheet. Alongside our studies, all students were encouraged to take part in community projects, showcases and huge college productions. Miss Archer actively invited me to channel my frustration at injustice and expand on my crazy ideas to make things right. That resulted in myself and two friends creating a touring show of thought-provoking musical comedy sessions on gender inequality at other colleges around the county. It gave me my first taste of real purpose outside of my own struggles.

High school had been the equivalent of having a bit part in a five-year version of *The Hunger Games*. One of the reluctant survivors whose instinct to fight has been embedded in them but they sway between continuing and wondering if it's worth carrying on. My teenage years had been an oppressive journey with too many potholes on the pavement that took all of my energy to avoid. And that left little headspace for finding the will to commit the events leading up to World War One to memory for the following week's test.

Once I got to college, there was a marked difference in how the staff related to the students. The most obvious being that they appeared less stressed! Some of that may have been down to the fact that we were older and actually wanted to be in education, most of us anyway, but the relationships were real. The tutors were authentic, and after an initial period of wariness (before logic kicked in and I realised how unlikely it was, and how much organisation it would take, for *all* of them to be punking me) I started to drop my guard a little.

I took everything personally and often assumed innocent comments were actual attacks. A friend and talented musician who had done nothing but show kindness to me turned up one day with a brand-new saxophone. She was incredibly excited and told me it had cost almost two grand. My response was bitter.

'What a waste. I could live for a year on that!' I hated myself for pouring cold water on her joy and lashing out in an attempt to mask my shame at the physical and mindset poverty I lived in. The guilt spiral began. I shouldn't even be here. I was asking for trouble by insisting on staying in full-time education rather than accepting the fact that people like me didn't do things like this. I should pack it in and settle for the same 'stealing and dealing' path as most of those I grew up around.

The societal system of the time just wasn't set up for someone like me to do something different. The government deemed me too young to be living independently and too old to be in foster care. I was advised by one official that I had two choices: go home and make amends with my parents or stop wasting time trying to get to university and take the first job I could find. I tried to explain that the first option wasn't viable and while I understood that the second was an acceptable route, I had already bust a gut getting to where I was and I wanted to follow through.

Some people praised me for trying to 'better' myself. I was just trying hard not to become bitter. Recently I was invited to speak at an event at the House of Lords on social mobility. I shared my thoughts on one of the issues people with my background have with the idea of upward social mobility (because it goes both ways, right?), that it's always assumed to be the highest and best goal to aim for. England even has a Tsar for it. One downside that the politicians don't tend to focus on is the actual cost to the better-ee.

For me, choosing to stay in education was expensive but not just financially. It was like I had climbed out of a particularly deep and difficult-to-scale pit before collapsing exhausted at the top and squinting in the bright light. My climb had been treacherous and as I stood in the sun with the first-time luxury of taking a look at myself, I noticed how filthy I was. With torn clothes, and drenched in my own sweat, tears and blood, I look back at those still in the pit and peer into the dark to see outstretched hands reaching up to me. My siblings! Suddenly, I forget the fatigue from years of climbing and I feel elated! This is it! This is the moment things change. The moment one of us, having 'escaped', gets to pull everyone else out. I reach down only to find that the hands were not reaching out to be pulled up but to pull me back in. Then I hear the refrain 'People like us don't do things like that.'

The choice is to return to the pit or walk away and leave your family, your community, all that you know. I can totally understand why people don't. A huge part of leaving/bettering myself meant forgoing a membership and never being able to return. It wasn't a trip to Narnia, it's a one-way passport-surrendering identity-abandoning ticket to the new world, baby! Sure, I could jump on a bus and travel to where I once lived but I'd no longer have the agreement from the community that I belonged. That in itself is a huge cherry on the chelsea bun but the real kicker is discovered later when you realise that no matter how long you live in your 'bettered-self', upwardly mobile, middle-class world, you'd never truly feel like you belong there either! You simultaneously know too much and too little about both sides to feel fully part of either. I'm no longer considered working class enough to be working class and I'm not middle class enough to get my head round buying sourdough bread from Waitrose!

I was surrounded by fabulous friends and terrific tutors at college, but I couldn't shake the loneliness I felt. I had what all my student friends wanted – parent-free independence. But what I craved was someone at home who, in a parenting role, would take an interest in me and support me, someone who would cajole, congratulate or commiserate with me. Someone outside of my own head who could offer me a different narrative than the one I told myself – that I was a fraud and would eventually be found out.

Dramarama

'You know you're good at leading others, yes?'

Miss Archer's question came out of nowhere. Before I could muster my usual self-deprecating response, she continued, 'We're starting a lunchtime drama group. You're running it.'

That's how she got me – no room for argument. Just like that, I was committed to showing up every Wednesday, rain or shine, whether I had eaten or not. The responsibility and her belief in me allowed me to be driven by something more powerful than hunger: she trusted me. She had more faith in me than I had in myself.

The first few sessions were basically chaos accompanied by a 1980s soundtrack. Miss Archer busied herself rearranging props around the sofas, keeping an eye on me while I facilitated the mayhem at the stage end of the hall. After letting me flounder a bit, she suggested exploring real emotions. The next week, I chose grief and loss – something I knew something about.

Then came the session that changed everything.

Miss Archer asked me to wait backstage while she 'demonstrated something'. Hidden behind thick black curtains, I waited, craning an ear to listen out for what she was saying. Is this where she apologises to the group for having landed them with such a useless tutor and says that she would be taking it from here?

'I have something to tell you,' her voice carried through the darkness. 'There's been an incident ... and well, she's gone.'

What was she on about? Who's gone? Where?

'She's passed away,' Miss Archer continued before describing someone remarkable. Someone who gave endlessly despite their own struggles. Someone who brought joy and encouragement to others' lives. Someone who had just died.

It was so convincing I wasn't sure if it was a workshop session or a real event. I wondered if I knew this girl too? Was she in my year? She sounded amazing.

Then Miss Archer said my name. That someone was me.

My head spun. Imagine hearing your own eulogy, but realising that you were still there, standing in the wings of your own life. How did she know what I was feeling? I mean, what was she going to say? The only thing stopping me from shame spiralling out of control was trying to get my head around the way she was describing me.

It was an uncomfortable listen. Praise still made me feel physically sick. Miss Archer was able to articulate deep emotions that I hadn't shared with her. She seemed to know feelings I thought I'd kept deeply hidden. As she described the truth about my life and lamented the tragedy of my death, she talked about the loss and what it would mean to all those whose lives I had touched. Miss Archer painted a picture of a young woman I didn't recognise but desperately wanted to be.[3] Then came the words that stopped my heart:

'It's heartbreaking... such a terrible waste, for her to end her own life like that.'

I froze.

Dread mingled with shame made me catch my breath.

How did she know?

The hall was silent but for a few stifled and shocked sobs. I was on high alert. Every fibre of my being had just been slapped awake. Imposter syndrome isn't a syndrome if you are an actual imposter – and I was – trying to be a student

---

[3] ... and still do! I'm not there yet, but now I have a fantastic role model. My phenomenal daughter Trinity is the woman I want to be when I grow up!

with a dream but inside feeling like a failure and longing after darkness. Did being found out mean that I'd be kicked out of college?

With that mic drop, Miss Archer stood, left the group of sobbing teenagers and exited stage left. As she passed me, still standing in the wings, our eyes locked. Mine full of fear and hers full of determination. I gripped the curtain for stability, she reached out and gripped my arm, forcing me to notice the pained emotion on her face.

'That's what the world looks like without you,' she whispered fiercely.

And leaving me with that truth bomb, she walked away.

Disorder in court

The amazing reframe I was receiving from Miss Archer, and college, was reshaping my worldview and my belief about what was possible, but my life outside of studying was still interrupting my attempts to escape its clutches. I was struggling to steer my way through the stress jungle of sitting my exams.

Hours before I took my first philosophy paper, I stood in a courtroom giving a particularly harrowing account in one of the many hearings for the court to decide if my siblings were safe with my parents or not. I stood in the witness box forcing myself to face the judge when answering questions and avoiding eye contact with my parents sitting a few feet away. Their solicitor, an expert witness badgerer, pursued a particularly sickening line of questioning:

> Him: 'You claim your stepfather had unwanted sexual contact with you.'
>
> Me: 'I don't claim it, it's the truth and he's already been found guilty …'
>
> Him: 'Yes or no will suffice.'
>
> Me: 'Yes.'
>
> Him: 'In fact, your own mother has shared that you were a sexually advanced child.'
>
> Me: 'What? No! That's ridiculous …'
>
> Him: 'That you were constantly initiating sexual contact …'

Me: 'No.'

Him: '... with your stepfather ...'

Me: 'No!'

Him: '... and other men who visited the home.'

Me: 'No! That's not true! I was six years old, for God's sake.'

At that point, the judge intervened to ask if I needed a break, but my biological mother put paid to that idea by letting go of my stepfather's hand to stand and scream at me, hurling phrases like 'selfish liar', 'black b*tch' and 'n*gger whore' before being escorted out of the courtroom.

It was a hugely destructive moment. I was being accused of lying by yet another adult, only this time in a courtroom in front of the perpetrator. The last tiny part of me that had hoped that my biological mother would hear what my stepfather had done and stand by me died during that hearing. I didn't think anything else she could say or do would hurt me more than she already had at that stage. I prided myself on not caring but it was yet another mask I wore to protect myself.

On the bus back to college I couldn't shake the thought that if the woman who gave birth to you thought so little of you how can you be worth anything at all? I made it to the exam, slapped my mask back on, smiled weakly at my friends and sat staring blankly at the paper. I managed to write some answers before it all got too much. I finished the paper by scrawling 'I am not enough' over and over again before laying my head on my hands to hide my pain and willing myself to sleep.

I sat all my exams but was woefully underprepared. University felt like a pipe dream at the beginning and was drifting even further into the distance. It only had a glimmer of a chance of happening when I held on to it tightly. Now I'd let go. I wanted to prove Miss Archer, Mr Simpson, Mr Williams and Mrs Cook right to have believed in me but never stopped worrying that they had been wrong.

Audacity in action

Just before I started the first term of college a social worker contacted me. She introduced herself as Sarah and explained that she was following up a concern raised by my younger brother's school and had dug into our family's records. Sarah explained she'd found my previous disclosures and floored me by actually apologising that they had not been acted upon.

She went on to prove that she could be trusted by finding a foster care placement for two of my younger brothers and switching the child benefit my parents were still claiming for Paul and my sister to my nan. While I was obsessed with getting my youngest brother adopted, she was keen that I also report the historical sexual abuse to the police.

Talking about what had been done to me was never easy. It didn't come with relief or release and going over it again and again only served to make the pain worse. Speaking out meant stripping myself bare, becoming more vulnerable than ever, and then sitting in the unbearable silence of *what happens next*.

In this case the next resulted in my stepfather being arrested, questioned and actually confessing! It took several more years but, eventually, all of my siblings were placed in long-term foster care or adopted.

None of the wins made me feel any better. I didn't know how to 'be'. My stepfather's court case was on the front page of the local paper and I couldn't speak for a week. I began to understand why so many victims of sexual assault and rape don't press charges. It can feel like being assaulted all over again just because you had the audacity to speak out.

If this is your story too – past or present – please read this next part twice:

> **The shame you carry is not yours. Find someone you trust and speak out.**[4]

I failed to achieve the A level grades I needed to accept my conditional offer at university.

I had worked hard – at surviving, at sticking with education, at holding it all together. I had given everything I could spare. I kept going when things felt

---

[4] For more information see https://www.nspcc.org.uk/preventing-abuse/signs-symptoms-effects/non-recent-abuse/ and the support section at the end of this book.

impossible. I had done everything that was expected of me and more. And it still wasn't enough.

My anguish at failing quickly turned inwards, morphing into more shame. How could I have been so stupid as to believe someone like me could get a place at university?

Calling every university in the country required more energy and hope than I had, but Miss Archer's pep talk got me home and sat by the phone.

Being audacious enough to try and try again (and then try pretending to be Scottish) had given me a second chance at a degree.[5] I agonised over what to do next and came pretty close to calling back to cancel the interview. Eventually, desperation won and I went all in, borrowing the train fare from one of the local dealers, knowing there was no way I'd be able to pay him back,[6] and caught a train. I knew I was just going to have to come clean about not being Scottish at all, oh and about having Es not As, but was struggling with how exactly to do that.

The best I could come up with was an apology and an explanation that I had been accidentally and temporarily Scottish in order to get the interview and convince them I was worth taking a chance on. It sounded more and more ridiculous the more I went over it in my head.

The interview room was a long thin space with a huge desk at the end. Behind the desk sat a man with an unruly mass of blond hair which looked as if a horse had been nibbling at it. He welcomed me in and before I had the chance to even start my absurd explanation as to why I'd suddenly lost my Scottish heritage, he jumped in ...

> **Him: 'Ahh, it's you. I have a couple of questions for you about where you live.'**
>
> **Me (*steeling myself but still stuttering*): 'Okay, erm well, erm ...'**

---

5   Of course, I'm not advocating lying about your grades, however, I don't think that pretending to be Scottish is lying, it's aspirational!

6   Appears reckless but shows my level of commitment. He had a strong working relationship with the local kneecapper so entering into any loan agreement meant you had to be dead sure either that you could pay it back – with extortionate interest – or that you were going to leave town for good.

Him: 'I have a family member who volunteered as a youth worker on your estate ...'

Me (*now dreading what he was about to say next and thinking about making a swift exit*): 'Riiiight ...'

Him: '... a few years back.'

Me (*Abort! Abort! Abort!*): 'Okay.'

Him: 'It's a challenging place to grow up, isn't it?'

Me (*wasn't expecting that – is it a trick question?*): 'Errrr, I suppose ...'

Him: 'From what I've heard it's rare for someone from your community to stay in education to this level. How did you make it this far?'

Me (*pausing for a split millisecond before seizing the opportunity to lay it all down*): 'Well, let me tell you a story ...'

I started speaking before realising that I didn't have the words to truly express just what it meant to be at that interview. Or what it would mean to be the first person in the history of my family to finish school let alone get to university and gain a degree. I had no way of defining how much it would mean to become like the teachers who, each in their own ways, had transformed a broken little girl into ... well, me.

It was a garbled jumble of a narrative heralding the four Everyday Heroes who had transformed my life to date. He sat and listened while I laid it all out for him. I can't remember the details I shared during that ten-minute tirade, but I remember it being the most emotion and gratitude filled plea I'd ever expressed.

When I finally took a breath and looked at him, I noticed his face now matched his hair – like a cartoon character in the aftermath of an ACME explosion. I instantly knew what to say, a sentence that would level out the conversation and bring the interview back down to earth. In one breath I fired out, 'And by the way, I was accidentally Scottish on the phone and I got two Es, not two As, is that okay?'

His innocent enquiry had unlocked a tornado of passion. It was the depth of gratitude I had for my teachers, the Everyday Heroes who had saved my life on so many occasions. What's more, it had an impact on him. His expression unfroze, he smiled and said, 'If you promise to be more authentic, I promise to do everything I can to get you on this course.'

I wasn't sure what 'being authentic' actually meant, but I figured that I could give it a go. It was probably easier than maintaining my totally unconvincing Scottish accent for four years.

That was the end of the interview and the beginning of my time at Bishop Grosseteste. I didn't know it yet but that was where I was to meet my fifth Everyday Hero. I left the interview and pegged it back to tell Miss Archer the good news and avoid bumping into the kneecapper-adjacent loan shark on the way.

Miss Archer's Legacy

Fear drove much of my behaviour during my years at college. I was an enormous, slimy alien uncomfortably squeezed into a human student-sized skin suit desperately pretending to be 'normal' so as not to alert the authorities.[7] I was terrified that someone would unzip the skin suit, peel it back and find the truth about me to be evident. I didn't belong. But Miss Archer was different – no frills, just facts. I loved that about her because I didn't have to waste precious energy trying to interpret what she actually thought by reading facial expressions or hunting for hidden meanings. I could just trust her words.

Miss Archer had this incredible ability to see straight through my defences. She'd catch me in the corridor between lessons and encourage me with a casual but solid statement. Before I could argue or deflect, she'd already moved on, leaving me to process the radical idea that I might actually have what it takes to succeed.

Being audacious is basically being 10% braver. Bravery is different to courage. Firefighters are courageous. They run towards danger while the rest of us run screaming in the opposite direction. Bravery is when you're terrified and you doubt yourself but still choose to take the first step.

---

7   Yes, I felt like I was Slitheen. I can neither confirm nor deny that I'm a massive *Star Trek* fan and slight *Doctor Who* geek.

Like Mr Simpson and Everyday Heroes everywhere, she was also consistent – a steady presence with encouragement-flavoured empathy. And, best of all, she didn't allow the challenges I faced to become a barrier to my capacity to grow. She talked about 'potential' rather than 'ability'. Not what I had done – or failed to do – but what I was capable of doing.

'When something is important,' she would tell me, 'you find a way.' This wasn't just a throwaway line – she lived it. She demystified the curriculum, allowing me to rail against the parts that seemed unfair, before zeroing back in on what mattered most. She had a talent for making her support feel like collaboration rather than charity.

What made Miss Archer extraordinary was her ability to hold space for both truth and possibility. One seemingly small thing I loved was that she always wrote her tutor comment on my end of term report directly to me, knowing that I had no parents to report to. She never minimised the reality of what I was dealing with, but she also refused to let me let it define me. When I'd try to use my circumstances as a reason why I couldn't do something, she'd listen with complete empathy, then simply ask, 'Okay, so how else can you approach this?'

I carried a raging sense of injustice with me in those days, masking it with self-deprecation and humour. I was terrified that if I failed even once to hold everything inside, if my distress leaked out in anything that could be mistaken for anger, I'd be done for, labelled an 'angry Caramel Taupe woman' at best, arrested at worst. Miss Archer encouraged me to channel that energy into creativity instead.

That drama club was more than just a weekly activity. While others might have been horrified by the reality of what I was dealing with, Miss Archer chose to stand with me in the chaotic fire that was my life. I wasn't the only student who Miss Archer inspired. In fact, when she retired a new theatre was built and named after her. Sure she had served the college well for several years, but to have a theatre named after you is a testament to the legacy of her own authenticity and the impact she had on everyone.

Back then it was audacious to believe anything other than the 'fact' that I was unworthy. Not only did Miss Archer support me then, she gave me a tool for navigating my way out of that belief in the future. Even today those thoughts still arise, but with more sophisticated outfits, like self-doubt and impostor syndrome. For example, after I won Speaker of the Year, I spent the whole year trying to convince myself of something that everybody else already knew. New information about yourself always requires you to upgrade the story you tell yourself about yourself, and as I've often been told, it's not bragging if it's true!

Through her consistency and belief, Miss Archer gave me something more powerful than escape – she gave me the tools to build a life that I didn't want to escape from. In short, Miss Archer taught me that self-esteem isn't something you earn through usefulness – it's your audacious birthright as a human being.

Be Miss Archer: Reflections

1. **Control the controllables**

    One of the most eye-opening activities in my interactive keynotes is inviting people to fill two circles. One with all the things you are in control of and the other with things you have no control over. Often it all boils down to the fact that the only thing we are in control of is the way we show up. Who's driving your bus? So many times I let fear of failure drive mine – often, ironically, straight towards a cliff edge! Don't waste your energy giving expletive-laden feedback to other drivers on the road. Focus on what you have the power to change. What one small thing can you take charge of today?

2. **Use desperation for inspiration**

    Miss Archer had the level of clarity usually reserved for people who've had a near death experience. She had no time for sweating over the small stuff as she was totally future focused. Rather than wait for defeat, she planned for roadblocks and always had an alternative route in mind. For her, resilience was a strategy, not a reaction. Avoid cracking under pressure by planning when you're calm. Plan an audacious response to a future challenge you know is coming.

3. **Be more chocolate Hobnob**[8]

    I've used biscuits to teach resilience in school ever since I saw Peter Kay's stand-up comedy comparing the lack of resolve of rich tea biscuits with the fortitude of the mighty chocolate Hobnob when dunked in your cuppa! Resilience isn't about avoiding the dunk – it's about refusing to crumble (and shouting 'Dunk me again!' when you come up for air). Think of one situation that's been testing your patience, confidence or calm lately. What's the chocolate Hobnob version of yourself going to do about it?

---

8   ... and less Lionel Rich-Tea!

4. **Stop apologising**

   Women, I'm looking at you especially here! Miss Archer was not a fan of people apologising – especially when it was for speaking up, standing out, or existing! Every time you unconsciously apologise when it's not your fault you're modelling to those around you that taking up space is a problem. What are you apologising for that doesn't need fixing? Stop saying sorry when someone else bumps into you. Stop deflecting when someone compliments you. Listen to your words and start catching yourself.

5. **Give yourself a kind kick up the bottom**

   There's a world of difference between calling yourself up and calling yourself out. Berating yourself isn't helpful and just encourages you to swallow shame. You can only achieve what you believe you deserve. What story are you telling yourself about what's possible? Take a short sharp visit to Scissorland and trim the negative self-talk. Start your reframe by completing your own, 'If I was truly committed ...' statement.

6. **Write your own eulogy**

   I'm on record saying I'm going to have a funeral before I die because if people are saying nice things about me, I want to be there to hear them! Stop living as if you have spare lives hanging up in the wardrobe and craft yours now while you're still here to make changes to it. Miss Archer's dramatic staging of my 'death' woke me up to the impact my absence would have. If someone were to describe your legacy today, what would they say? What would you want them to say instead? You still have time to close that gap.

7. **Create your own sanctuary**

   Those hideous yet perfect sofas in Miss Archer's theatrical junk shop were my safe haven. It was something about sofas indicating home and my body would start relaxing as soon as I entered the hall and saw them at the other end. Where are you creating spaces that tell people 'It's okay to not be okay here'? In what ways could your classroom, office, or home become someone's life-changing sanctuary?

8. **Update your failure CV**

   My two Es felt like certification of my worthlessness, but became the foundation of my most powerful story. Consider your mistakes and write down the first three failures that spring to mind. Now, right next to each one, write what you've learned as a result. You've survived 100% of your worst days and acknowledging that will fortify you, making you stronger and more prepared for the next challenge.

9. **Get some SWAG**

   That's your Seriously Wild Audacious Goals. I'm not talking about an extra hour to try and get to inbox zero. Make sure you have one that is sufficiently serious, wild and audacious. If it doesn't make you have a little bit of sick come up in the back of your throat, you're not trying hard enough.

10. **Channel your inner Miss Archer**

    Whose potential can you see more than they can themselves? Miss Archer held a vision of success for me long before I had any concept of being able to do that for myself. She didn't just tell me – she created concrete opportunities for me to prove it to myself. Who around you needs a non-negotiable invitation to step into their potential?

Mr Readman
The One Who Taught Me Compassion

'You've changed.'

Two words that felt like a slap in the face.

I could see Paul standing behind me in the kitchen before he even spoke. My teenage brother had a way of entering a room like a ninja. He stood at the door, maintaining a distance that implied I was contagious. I turned, still clutching the bread knife I'd used to slice the loaf into two components of a doorstep sandwich, and attempted to break the tension with humour.

He didn't bite.

Paul, still short for his age, had grown into a teenager and simultaneously withdrawn from the world. He rarely left his room, having painted all four walls black, grown his hair long and given up on education providing a way through. He loved listening to thrash metal and only emerged from his bedroom in search of food.

I'd changed? What about him? He'd morphed into a miserable teenage Jesus lookalike[1] but, unlike Jesus, he seemed to be angry at everything and everybody, including me.

Paul didn't appreciate my critique of his appearance. Tensions rose quickly and the conversation took a turn onto a full-blown screaming match.

'All you ever do is leave! You said you'd get a job and buy a big house and we'd all live there. You lied and now you're leaving us.'

And there it was. The hope I'd injected into hopelessness. The promise I'd made and failed to keep. He told me that going away to university had turned me into a snob – the worst of all insults to throw at a working-class girl. We threw insults back at each other, but his first sentence was the one that stuck.

---

1 I know Jesus wasn't as pale as a pint of full-fat milk with greasy long blondish hair, but he was according to the pictures that decorated my Church of England high school. Paul bore a striking resemblance to the one hanging outside the teachers' smoking lounge.

'You've changed.'

With my usual lack of compassion, I'd deflected the guilt I felt straight back at him. In truth he was right. I hadn't rescued anyone, I'd escaped[2] and left them behind.

Hope is not a strategy

The last time I wanted to die was in my first year of university.

On the one hand, I'd done what felt like the impossible and made it on to a degree course. I was the first in my family to actually finish school, let alone get to university. I'd overcome so much and, on paper, was a bit of a poster girl for the UK education system. On the other hand, well, I was quite simply exhausted.

Any success was married with struggling under the weight of being a survivor. It sounds slightly ungrateful reading it written down and my non-compassionate pre-therapy self would definitely be telling me to: 'Pull yourself together! Everything is alright now so stop droning on about your *X Factor* back story. Nobody cares. Just get on with it.' Looking back, I had all the markers of post-traumatic stress. Vivid flashbacks, intrusive thoughts, night terrors, a barrage of constant negative emotions like fear, guilt, anger and shame and feeling totally detached from my surroundings had become a way of being for me.

The turning point was waking up in my halls on the morning after the end of yet another toxic relationship with some guy I'd allowed to treat me like crap. I was angry, at myself, at him, at the world.

Waking up even more heavy hearted than usual, I rationalised I was tired of being tired. I sat bolt upright and inside me a declaration formed. It was a rallying cry of someone who had tried to compromise themselves to the point of non-existence only to be constantly told they were still either 'too much' or 'not enough'. I was flat. I had literally turned the volume down on myself to nothingness and was living outside my own integrity and values.

---

2   That's the wrong word. You don't 'escape' a childhood or any form of trauma. It travels with you, even when the circumstances have changed. With help it is totally possible to process it and stop the past from haunting your present or impacting your future.

'If I'm going to be on this planet, there's going to be some changes around here!'[3]

Only one problem. How?

Enter Mr Readman, stage left.

A Whole New World (but not in a Disney's *Aladdin* sort of way)

In the early 1990s, diversity in education was transitioning from a 1980s focus on multiculturalism to considering deeper questions around belonging, bias and barriers. In larger cities and towns, with more variety of humans, these conversations were louder. In smaller towns with less representation, it was more of a whisper. I stepped into teacher training during what felt like an illusion of inclusion compared to today.

Lincoln felt safe and respectable in comparison with where I'd grown up. It teemed with tons of history, including a castle and a cathedral within spitting distance of each other. My university was a small college at the top of an unnecessarily steep hill. Before the bigger University of Lincoln was built, uni life was limited to the few hundred students who were either training to be teachers or attending agricultural college.

Away from my own school I'd often experienced being the 'only one' in classrooms. My foster placements tended to be in areas more affluent than the under-resourced inner-city area I lived, with very few brown faces. My teachers and tutors had been exclusively white throughout my own education but now the difference I'd navigated my whole life became more pronounced. I experienced random racism in the streets for the first time since the 1970s. It was confusing and embarrassing being shouted at while walking with friends but still better than experiencing it alone.

Much of the socialising was done on campus as there was a limited choice of only two nightclubs in town. Being in a club was akin to being an exhibit. I lost count of the amount of people who reached out to touch my hair as if I was a

---

3 Drastic change is triggered by inspiration or desperation. I had a tendency to wait for the latter.

passing cat inviting a stoke. Guys were curious about my heritage and keen to chat:

'You're quite exotic aren't you.'

'I've never been with a Black girl before …'

'You *must* be into Reggae?'

'You look like <insert any famous brown female here>.'

Meanwhile, I was consumed with trying to hide the poverty I'd experienced, my class and the fact that I'd been in foster care and didn't have a family at home to return to during the holidays. In general, the vibe was 'We treat everyone the same', which translated as 'We expect you to fit in with us.' I didn't have white privilege but I found myself being afforded 'white-adjacent privilege' – all I had to do to keep it was to be grateful, wind my neck in and keep my gob shut.

The UK education curriculum continued to be predominantly Eurocentric. Black History Month was in its infancy and my lectures contained very few mentions of diversity or trauma-informed pedagogy. I found myself code-switching like a pro and smiling through unintended microaggressions before I even knew those terms existed. Instead, I internalised my experiences as something I was causing in some way. On teaching practice, when one head cheerily explained: 'We've got one like you here, but he's no trouble.' I just smiled weakly.

Keeping my gob shut proved difficult. I failed in one of my first lectures where the lecturer playfully complained about us all sitting at the back so he could only see 'a hundred white blurs!' Equally playfully I replied, 'And one brown blur!' The result was a muffled titter followed by a silence akin to one of those 1950s cowboy films when a stranger walks into the saloon and the piano stops mid note.

Sitting through lectures about what children needed in education – while carrying my own childhood secrets in what felt like a huge rucksack – increased my sense of being an imposter. I tried not to squirm and give myself away while lecturers talked about the theory of the trauma I had experienced. I tried to make myself professionally small by swallowing my lived experience.

I was a fish out of water. Not quite belonging in this new academic sea, terrified I'd be spotted flapping about on the shore and be thrown back, only to find I'd forgotten how to swim.

The teacher training I received at Bishop Grosseteste was second to none. I applied the rigour and expertise that I developed over my four years of training every year in every role since. Even with my own shortcomings, that course set me up to be a fantastic teacher. My problem was a lack of confidence and inability to ask for help. I was embarrassed by my lack of basics. We were told that skirts must be worn during teaching practice. My entire wardrobe consisted of three pairs of leggings and two lumberjack shirts. I spent the week of my first teaching practice wearing a lycra body con mini dress pulled down to my hips hoping that the jumper I borrowed from my neighbour covered the shoulder straps hanging down at the sides.

University offered a new start, but I was overwhelmed and unprepared for the practicalities of student life. When my dormmates started packing up their rooms for the Christmas break, I panicked. Without a family home to return to I had assumed I would be able to stay in my university accommodation. I'd used humour and bravado to hide my fear of not belonging and general anxiety, but once I discovered that the security of a roof over my head was temporary, it started to fade. I enquired about the possibility of staying in halls alone during the holidays with the head of pastoral care. I didn't want to give all the details and struggled to answer his query about why I couldn't just return to my parents. He advised me that my unique circumstance was something I should have considered before applying for a degree.

Too embarrassed/stupid to ask for help from anyone in my hometown I ended up that first night sleeping in the doorway of what was then the Department for Social Security with two bin bags of clothes and posters I'd taken down from my walls. My student finance didn't cover food or accommodation in the breaks so finding paid employment during the holidays consumed my term time brain, with studying squeezed in around the edges. I struggled to focus and couldn't seem to finish any of my assignments until the deadline loomed. It seemed I was only able to function when under extreme stress. Surviving from one term to the next became the main driver for me and explains my fantastic 'Failure CV'! I had a myriad of jobs: handing out leaflets in the street, cleaning pubs, being a chambermaid, driving/cooking for a family of eight in remote northern Scotland,[4] dancing in a cage wearing a white catsuit and a Miss Malibu sash in a nightclub, and facepainting on a ferry.

The gap between starting holiday jobs and waiting to be paid risked hunger and homelessness. Luckily, the skills I'd learned surviving as a kid in foster care and on the streets are very similar to the skills needed to be an entrepreneur. I worked out that I would make more money by cutting out the middleman and becoming one of those self-employed clowns you hear so much about. It's amazing how innovative you can become when you're desperate.

---

[4] Having just passed my test, my driving was lousy but better than my cooking. However, the job meant six weeks of accommodation, so I aced the interview, and the *Good Housekeeping Cookbook* became my new best friend.

Apart from being hired for general clowning, I put my teaching skills to good use and set up my own little circus school. I made juggling balls out of balloons and pearl barley, writing out 'How to juggle' instructions by hand (photocopying them cost an extortionate 10p a time). Then, standing in the street, I sold my 'Jazzy Jugglers' with a promise to teach any customer how to juggle in fifteen minutes or less or their money back!

Thankfully things are very different today. Bishop Grosseteste University has a huge focus on social purpose with equality and diversity at the centre of that. It doesn't shy away from the courageous conversations needed in this space and has a reputation for pastoral care. Like most universities today, it now offers specific support packages for those who are care experienced, including year-round accommodation, additional financial support and mentoring.

> **If you're estranged from your parents or care experienced yourself and worried how you would navigate the challenges of being at university – reach out. Your resilience is not just valid – it's incredibly valuable. The very survival skills you've built navigating life so far are the same strengths that will carry you through your studies. Not only do you belong in those lecture halls, you have something unique that others without your experience lack. Be how I wish I'd been brave enough to be back then. There is support out there – financial, emotional, and practical – and there are people who genuinely want to see you win. You are not alone.**

A difference in teaching styles

During that first year of university, I hated myself for not 'getting it'. I was trying so very hard to appear acceptable and convince myself I had every right even to be there. All the time I lived with this intense and crippling fear of being found out. I worried what would happen to me if it was discovered that I wasn't 'one of them'. If there was one survival strategy I was convinced of, it was that success relied on my ability to make myself invisible and blend in. It was unfortunate that I had a history of being rubbish at both.

Being a chaos navigator who had made it to the other side of the tracks gave me a different insight to the one I was presented. Of course, the lecturers were not immune to discussing the impact of growing up in an under-resourced community. One even described herself as an expert, and I was excited to attend her sessions. Her view of 'the poor disadvantaged kids' wasn't quite on a par with what I had experienced. I wanted to share that the reality for some children and families was more stark than that and the power that we had as teachers to change lives was hugely impactful.

Being schooled on poverty felt like being a native Spanish speaker living in Margate and sat in a Year 7 Spanish lesson when the teacher's off sick, and a passing parent on a tour of the school reckons they can have a go because they've been to Benidorm a couple of times.

My attempts to engage in the debate were clumsy and riddled with a persecution complex. The more successful steps I took in my education journey, the more of an undeserving imposter I felt. I wanted validation. I wanted someone to tell me it was okay and it didn't matter if my starting point was different, I still had plenty to offer the profession. I wanted to speak up but also thought it best to stay under the radar and avoid drawing attention to myself. I couldn't give myself away, too much was riding on me not being found out.

I'd formed the belief that the system valued surface-level knowledge more than the raw understanding of lived experience. That belief added to my intense fear of being found out. On one occasion I plucked up the courage to tell a visiting tutor that my goal was to teach children facing the challenges of living in under-resourced communities. The tutor told me I was naive, had 'a lot to learn about "disadvantaged" children' and that it would require a special kind of teacher to cope in that environment. I was conflicted. Do I celebrate my success at blending in and not being recognised as one of those kids? Or do I speak up on behalf of them and reveal who I really am?

A sentence in a lecture made my mind up for me. 'All parents care deeply about their child's education.' I knew this not to be true. Not only that, but it was also an unhelpfully inaccurate assumption. Such thinking had been a major factor in the neglect and abuse I experienced from my parents remaining undiscovered. Panic set in. If we send teachers out into schools believing that *all* parents care, what about when they don't? What if history repeats itself? What will those teachers believe when a child presents them with a different reality?

I was spiralling. With trauma, when you're triggered, your nervous system can't always tell the difference between what was *then* and what is *now*. You can be sat in a meeting wearing a suit but suddenly feel as vulnerable as when you were five years old. Or feel like you're back in that bedroom, even though you're an adult standing in your own kitchen clutching a tin of tuna. Trauma disrupts timelines and causes you to overreact, shutdown or struggle with memories so vivid they feel more like a 6D movie experience. Within milliseconds your amygdala fires up and screams 'danger' as if the threat was real rather than imagined, remembered or perceived, and, bingo, you're in flight, flight or freeze mode.

Rationally, I knew swapping judgement for curiosity results in more impact than railing against those with different opinions to your own. I wasn't in rational mode. Ever seen *Les Misérables*?[5] There's a bit in it where the main man, Jean Valjean has the chance to escape scot-free because the authorities have caught someone they think is him. 'Who am I?' he asks, as he battles with his conscience. Do I keep my head down and let an injustice come to pass? But, if I speak, I am condemned. Is this what I've become?[6]

While my life was certainly no musical, I was going through a similar battle there and then in that lecture theatre. Is my degree a chance to pretend my past never happened? Or am I here because I wanted to take any and every opportunity to be the voice of those who went unheard?

I looked around the room. I saw my peers and the potential they held to be the Everyday Heroes just like the ones who transformed my life. I thought about the reason I had come into teaching in the first place and raised my hand.

Lecturer: 'Yes?'

Me: 'That's not entirely true. Some parents don't care about their children, let alone their education ...'

Looking at it from her point of view, I was contradicting her for no apparent reason other than to interrupt. She asked for my name, which is what people do when they either want to be friends or are mentally adding you to their list of annoying humans.

I gave her my name which she used as a fronted adverbial in her next sentence explaining why I was wrong.

'No, I'm not,' I replied cantankerously. I was cross at the adults who had failed to hear me in the past but for reasons I didn't fully understand myself, in that moment, directed it at her.

She doubled down. 'In my thirty years of experience, I've never met a parent who didn't care deeply about their child's education!' I found myself in the

---

5   I haven't, but every person I know on the planet has, and they have all, at one time or another, recounted the entire plot to me, complete with musical numbers and dance moves.

6   Spoiler alert: they all die. Also, it's Gwyneth Paltrow's head in a box at the end of *Seven*.

middle of a very public argument that I didn't actually want to be any part of even though I'd started it myself. I sat down.

After the lecture, the tutor called me over to let me know that I had a problem with authority – which wasn't news to me. It had been a common diagnosis for my behaviour throughout my time as a child and teenager but never came with any form of solution I could work on to have less of a problem with authority. I lowered my head, swallowed my question and apologised.

Outside the lecture theatre another tutor stopped me and asked me why I'd spoken up. It stopped me in my tracks, realising I was stood in front of a potential Category 1 adult. His compassion melted my indignation in the dispassionate, disassociated manner that I had perfected by now to save both the listener and me from embarrassment and awkwardness. We stood on the path and had an amazing conversation. I gave the gentle tutor a sanitised version of what caused me to speak up and how much of a debt I owed to educators.

He smiled and nodded while I spoke and when I finished, he told me that the course was like an apple: 'You eat the good and spit out the bad.'

If he'd shown any signs of pity or saviour-seeking behaviour, I would have thrown back 'Yeah, but I've got to sit through four years of this crap! That's a lot of apple spitting.' Instead, I paused. Who do I want to be? What did I want more? For things to change for the better or to argue my point to death in an attempt to be 'right'? It's a question I still use to guide me today. Most of the time there isn't a perfect answer but I'm learning that just by asking it, it gives you more insight and helps you to dig a lot deeper and get closer to the truth.

It was interactions like this that taught me I did have a problem. I started to understand that, in actual fact, my 'you don't know what it's like' stock response showed a total lack of compassion and empathy for anyone with a different experience to mine – the very shortcoming of which I was accusing them.

The gentle tutor stood in the quad, positioning himself between me and the canteen where lunch was beckoning. Without any big ceremony or fanfare, he reached into his tweed jacket pocket and took out something small – a book of postage stamps.

'Stay connected to those who love you,' he said handing me the gift – today's equivalent of someone handing you an iPad. With a kindness that still takes my breath away, he interrupted the isolation I felt and made me feel seen.

Years later, when I found myself able to offer similar kindnesses, I often thought of him. That small act of compassion, and countless others I received along my journey, strengthened me then and continues to today.

Finding a home in Hull

My first year was tough but my second year, at Hull University, saw a marked uptick in life becoming easier.

As a bigger city, Hull was more dynamic and diverse than Lincoln. It also had a huge heart. It was proud of its working-class industrial foundation but also aware of the economic benefit an influx of students could bring. I was much less of a minority and belonged to a huge student community.

I became a proud member of the Piper's Club in its original form as a working men's club. It was a smoke-filled paradise of pipe-smoking men that reminded me of my grandad. Activities included bingo with the prize of a tray of cellophane-wrapped raw meat from the local butcher! Students were welcomed as long as they paid the 20p entrance fee and didn't mind the doorman confiscating any bibles at the door![7] People tended to speak their mind, live and let live or simply keep themselves to themselves. It was like the early days living with my nan and grandad.

Hull University holds a special place in my heart. It was the setting for a transformative chapter in my young adult life – a chapter that not only elevated my education but expanded my mind and my sense of self. The year I transferred to Hull, something shifted and clicked into place. I studied drama – exploring stories of people outside of my experience and widening my garden of possibility. It helped that the city saw students as an integral part of it rather than passing visitors. I relaxed into my new surroundings for the first time in a long time, and in doing so, I found something I hadn't even realised I still longed for – a sense of home.

Opting to stay during the Christmas break, I approached the local shopping centre and offered to juggle and paint faces inside where it was warm. The manager agreed, for only 10% of my profit, and brought his own kids to have their faces painted twice in one day! I was highly motivated, and my confidence grew with every paying customer. One passing mum asked me if I did children's parties.

> **External voice:** 'Yes, madam, I most certainly do!'
>
> **Internal voice:** 'I do now! How hard can it be?'

---

7   Community was big in Hull and local churches drew crowds of students by providing Sunday lunch free of charge every week!

A quick visit to a junkyard meant I had enough pipes and tubes to attach to some old overalls and, with the addition of a spray can of silly string, I became the first female 'Ghostbuster' (in your face, Melissa McCarthy!). I turned up at the gig on a bike I'd rescued from a skip complete with a bag full of ectoplasm (made from flour, water and green food colouring). In this manner, the holidays were tiring, but it was also immensely satisfying to be sustaining myself and getting through the days so that I could get back to fulfilling my dream.

Looking back, I now realise that, in order to survive, my drive was in overdrive. I saw threats everywhere (hunger, homelessness, being found out, not being good enough, worrying about my siblings, running out of pearl barley for my Jazzy Jugglers ...) and my response was to work harder, push further, fight hard and fight even harder.

Every set back – and there were plenty – required more innovation, forging a way through the adversity. I wasn't big on self-care, so although I kept going, and managed to continue to support myself through the first two years of my four-year degree, it was a hugely unhealthy short-term strategy for existing.

All of that was about to change. Back in Lincoln for my third year, I met the newly appointed Head of Drama in Education, Mr Readman – a special kind of human who helped me to direct my attention towards investing in compassion and care for myself.

The re-storying begins

Despite the belonging I'd found, Paul's words wouldn't let go.

By my third year, the fight that was staying in university education started to lose its attraction. What was the point of trying to help other children when I had failed the ones I considered to be my own? As I prepared to leave Hull and return to Lincoln for the start of the new term, a familiar darkness had descended over me and the thought of graduating no longer seemed possible. I soothed myself by saying that one day, when my siblings became adults, I'd sit them down and explain everything and they would understand. One day.

In the meantime, I lost my passion for survival and saw little point in wrecking myself for a third year in the vain hope I'd make it through and get my teaching degree. What state would my brothers and sister be in then?

I was already in more debt than I could ever imagine repaying. My life started a familiar spiral and, once again, I focused on ways to punish and destroy myself for being stupid enough to dream I could be anything more than a worthless street kid.

This was the defeated young human female Mr Readman encountered. It didn't appear to faze him in the slightest. Mr Readman was unwaveringly excited about the positive impact his subject, and our grasp of it, could bring to education. He was all about people and showed me how to start the slow painstaking process of replacing my anger with optimism and my hopelessness with expectations of possibility. He helped me understand that it wasn't always about winning or losing or success or failure but rather about embracing an unerringly optimistic belief that change was possible when taken one slow, incremental, caring step at a time.

Mr Readman helped me uncover one of my superpowers – pivoting and reframing. The ability to meet a roadblock and quickly find a positive, productive and beneficial way round. With this power, whatever happened could become something I was able to use to move me forward.

I was frustrated with life, tired of trying and masking deep sadness and unprocessed trauma with humour in public and self-loathing in private. I'd come so far, surviving a particularly brutal round of Monopoly and was sitting on the last Community Chest space before passing Go and finally collecting that £200. At only halfway through my degree, I knew there was capacity for further disaster but wasn't sure I had the strength to survive it.

Yet everything Mr Readman taught me had compassion at its core – compassion for others and, of huge importance, compassion for self. Trying to hold anger and compassion at the same time is like trying to whistle the national anthem while drinking a pint of Vimto. You have to choose. Compassion appears counterintuitive when you're in pain, but choosing it enables you to meet people where they are. And then they actually start to listen. Really listen. This revelation changed everything.

Mr Readman helped me embark on a ten-year journey. Even with all the reading, healing, therapy, coaching and all the work I went on to invest my time and energy in, it still took me years. But it started with this real shift in terms of self-compassion and forgiveness. Mr Readman modelled professional vulnerability and personal authenticity. Our conversations were run through with

'with-ness', agency and a sure and certain belief in my potential. I couldn't do it all alone but he let me know he would be flying alongside me offering support and challenge with unconditional positive regard. To Mr Readman, he was simply doing his job. To me he was an actual bona fide hero. An Everyday Hero.

Mr Readman was an expert story weaver, unconcerned with status or a desire to be in control. He would invite us to actively drive our own learning bus rather than be compliant (or complaining) passengers. In his sessions, not only was belonging a fundamental part of the process, he also made sure there were no barriers to entry. I could join and contribute because it was okay to be me.

Once a feeling of safety and trust had been established, we then had the chance to explore complex issues. He encouraged us to do this by inviting us into courageous conversations through real stories about the human condition that required risk taking in the search for answers. Rather than entering a lecture theatre with my habitual baseline of fear – fear of being found out, fear of not blending in, fear of being wrong, fear of being praised – I started each session with the nervous excitement that comes from exploring unknown territory from a position of security.

In a way, I still can't explain – was it because I was older? Was it because I was so low that any encouragement to look up was invaluable? Mr Readman's drama inputs gave me the strongest sense in my education so far that I had something unique to offer the world. That my scars were in fact superpowers. I was valuable, and considered an equal. An equal? Imagine that for a moment. To be both valuable and valued at the same time.

You may not have experienced the sort of childhood where being treated as someone who has something to say, someone who matters, is such a rare treat. However, you do know what it's like to feel like the odd one out, to be unheard, to feel powerless. After so many years of silently screaming to be heard, actually being seen and listened to is exhilarating.

Utterly. Beautifully. Transformational.

I had dismissed history as a subject having spent more time outside the lesson than in it at high school. Now, through my drama in education sessions, I was introduced for the first time to the lives of pioneering people of colour like Harriet Tubman, Mary Seacole and Minik Peary Wallace.[8] It was the first time I'd

---

8   You have – I hope – heard of Harriet Tubman and Mary Seacole, but perhaps not Minik Wallace. Now that's a story to get your teeth into. Think about the questions that came into my head as I learned about his short life. How did he feel, for example, about being a live exhibit at the American Museum of Natural History? How did the staff justify to themselves faking his father's funeral, then putting his skeleton on display right next to Minik? What was the change of heart that led to the curator of the museum adopting Minik?

been introduced to brown historical figures – even the illustrations of Egyptians in my school history books had been the colour of scrambled egg!

I loved Mr Readman's invitation to ask better questions. He encouraged us to swap any judgement for curiosity when it came to the stories of others and to question everything we thought we were sure of and to find new ways to think about the world. For him, knowing what our core purpose or 'why' was had to be the first step before we embarked on any activity, lesson or even life decision. A big enough 'why' will drive you forward when things get sticky. He removed shame and fear by opening the door to a more unsanitised and raw version of history than I had experienced. One that explored the different responses of the few who were hurt by the many. The stories provided road maps for my own healing.

I was still unforgiving towards myself and made a lot of mistakes. My powers of observation combined with a strong sense of justice and the proven inability to opt for using my 'inside voice' meant that I was never far away from being the fly in someone's jammy doughnut. For example, when I read the articles and research papers required for my course, children were almost exclusively referred to as 'he' and 'him'. What with it not being 1492 and it being generally acknowledged that women did in fact exist, I brought it up with a tutor. When I raised the Great Prejudiced Pronoun Problem, he explained that the authors had obviously used 'he' to represent 'she' as well. I argued that an update in the language we used as educators was due but it was suggested that using anything other than male pronouns would be distracting for the reader!

In contrast, Mr Readman's sessions were established with equity in mind right from the get go. It was weirdly refreshing to have embedded micro barriers to the curriculum removed so quickly and easily and suddenly to be able to simply start exploring alongside everyone else – *as if* I was one of them. He then introduced us to powerful and challenging narratives that helped us think about our own lives. In this way, we learned that the stories we tell can have tremendous influence on the stories others tell about themselves, especially the children and young people we would be teaching.

A message in the real-life stories we explored with Mr Readman that kept rising to the top was that your past neither defines nor determines your future. What lay ahead of me was not going to be determined by what lay behind me. Hold onto that next time you hear the misinformed narrative that children who have been poorly parented end up as poor parents themselves, that children who ended up in care produce children who end up in care, that the abused end up as abusers. If I had a pound for every time I'd had this concept of apples not falling far from trees explained to me by a well-meaning expert, I'd have a lot of pounds.

Of course, there are examples where that is the case, plenty of them. But that doesn't make it a wrought iron cast in stone larger than life truth. Look at me. I'm a million miles away from being regarded as the gold standard of human but I've worked incredibly hard to ensure that one thing I am not and will never, ever, be is who my parents were. Way before the moment I knew I was going to become a mother myself, I committed to being the adult I needed as a child. That happened as a direct result of forgiving myself – something made possible by the foundation Mr Readman laid.

Mr Readman wrapped my experience in a new and more compelling story and allowed me to see myself as a healing human, not a walking time bomb. Thanks to the reframe I experienced studying drama with Mr Readman I began to see myself not as a victim, but as someone who had experienced victimisation. Thanks to his artful, engaging and life-affirming training, I learned about rewriting my own limiting narratives through the safe exploration of other people's stories. In his teaching, he made it clear that if you became curious, asked questions and embraced the opportunity to make different choices, then you got to be any type of human you wanted to be in the story you were writing.

As with most students, some of the people I met at university became lifelong friends yet, perhaps without realising it, they were also my stand-in family too. I borrowed their clothes, ate their food and on one occasion was almost officially adopted by someone's parents! I'm still in awe of and incredibly grateful to Manda, Elly, Ali, Mel, Amanda, Rob, Chris and so many others who opened their hearts, homes and families to me. Those friendships have sustained me and were a contributing factor to me never taking the idea of completing my course for granted. Over time I learned to trust and accept the love, kindness and generosity of others without guilt for not deserving it or suspicion that it was a trap!

So let me be really clear about this universal truth:

> **Your past is not a script for your future.**
>
> **Your future is a blank page and the pen is in your hand. As I say on stage – this is what it looks like on the other side of healing. And it's entirely possible for you too.**

Performance and forgiveness

Under Mr Readman's wing, I wrote my final year performance piece – a play called 'Stolen', exploring the impact of childhood abuse. Thinking back to that decision now, it was a first step towards the end of hiding and fear. I was deeply terrified of what people would think of me if they found out about my past. Up until then I'd carried it like a deeply shameful secret. The compassion that Mr Readman embedded in every session had seeped into the deepest part of my bones where the secret lived and softened the fear.

Being both brown and female (at the same time) were impossible to hide but my biggest struggle was technically the easiest to hide – being a foster care kid from the poorer end of working class who had experienced neglect and abuse. I experienced the discomfort of the social mobility path I was on and it was uncomfortable to suddenly find myself on the other side of the fence. The student body was heavily weighted towards adults who had been looked after as children rather than looked-after children, but we spent time in classrooms with children whose background I had much more in common with. I missed middle-class nuances but felt at ease with children who struggled to regulate their emotions. The play was a chance to speak confidently about an area I understood.

The CDC-Kaiser Permanente adverse childhood experiences (ACE) study[9] had not made it onto our reading list. While poverty was referred to in my lectures, abuse, domestic violence and neglect were not. Hardly anyone showed up to audition for my play and I faced questions about whether the unsavoury subject of my piece was appropriate. My confidence was knocked and those familiar feelings of fear and shame raised their head again. Should I 'just be quiet', 'stop making a fuss' and stick to retelling more palatable stories than my own?

Then a fourth year (and one belonging to the effortless cool student collective I could only ever aspire to being a member of!) turned up at the second round of auditions. I was confused – she was the equivalent of Beyoncé queuing up for the first round of *America's Got Talent*.

---

[9] V. J. Felitti, R. F. Anda, D. Nordenberg, D. F. Williamson, A. M. Spitz, V. Edwards, M. P. Koss and J. S. Marks, Relationship of Childhood Abuse and Household Dysfunction to Many of the Leading Causes of Death in Adults: The Adverse Childhood Experiences (ACE) Study, *American Journal of Preventive Medicine*, 14(4) (1998): 245–258. Available at: https://www.ajpmonline.org/article/s0749-3797(98)00017-8/pdf.

I began to explain what the play was about. When I'd finished she shared a little of her own story, including the sexual abuse from her own father. I was gobsmacked. It was my first actual conversation with another survivor. One of the tragedies of abuse is that the abused tend to steal the shame from the perpetrator and make it theirs. Shame breeds silence. Only that day, the silence between two friends was broken and a new and deeper connection and understanding was forged.

Take a bow

On the opening night of my play, Mr Readman stood at the back of the audience. The ending was especially poignant and as the metaphorical curtain fell, there was silence. No one said anything. Not a word. You could hear a pin drop, the pin that was probably about to burst my bubble.

Then suddenly, one lone clapper began a round of thunderous applause which encouraged others to join in. Mr Readman, hands above his head, with a huge grin on his face, beaming the biggest, proudest smile.

Every performance of my show was packed with people, crammed in and breaking several fire regulations. On the final night word had spread and many of the tutors attended. Afterwards I had several letters from student and staff audience members sharing their own stories, and congratulating me for my bravery and sensitivity. Later, Mr Readman told me I had taken brokenness and turned it into something powerful. But the truth is, I only got there because he stood with me. In the fire. Without flinching.

That's who he was.

He taught me to be compassionate by demonstrating compassion towards me. Rather than pulling me out of the storm or sheltering me from it, he simply walked beside me – soaked and steadfast – confident I could weather it. Believing I could find my footing.

His style was quiet, steady, undramatic. He'd nudge you toward something courageous, then take two steps back so the spotlight would fall entirely on you. He didn't need the glory. He already knew how the story ended.

And when it did, he'd be standing at the back of the room applauding like his life depended on it with that smile that told you: *You did it. I always knew you would.*

Because of him, I stopped seeing myself as a mistake.

Because of him, I began the lifelong journey of loving the parts of me I thought were unlovable.

Because of him, I live and tell a better story.

Because of you, Mr Readman.

Because of you.

Graduation Day

I stood outside Lincoln Cathedral looking up at its towers soaring into the sky. I'd learned a fair bit about that building and even given tours to unsuspecting tourists. Now I was standing outside with the wind whipping my robes around my legs. About to graduate. About to take flight.

I considered doing a cartwheel as I travelled across the stage to collect my rolled-up scroll. When my name was finally called, a cocktail of disbelief and relief swarmed in my chest and I walked towards the golden key I was about to receive to my future.

I accepted my certificate with shaking hands and just about managed to stop myself from hugging the presenting officer. I'd begun my time in Lincoln feeling like I was living someone else's life. Like I'd slipped through a door that wasn't meant for me and was waiting for someone to tap me on the shoulder and say, 'Sorry, love, this isn't yours.'

Four years later I was leaving not just with a deeply robust, fiercely valuable teacher training under my belt, but with a new story. A story rooted not in fear, but in belonging.

Taking a deep breath, I joined in the obligatory group cap toss. I watched it fly up into a sky thick with mortarboards as time seemed to slow to a momentary stand still. The caps seemed to hover, suspended in midair and defying gravity as if the universe was pausing just long enough to say: *Yes. This. This is what's possible.*

It was more than tradition. It was a declaration of fact. A story rewritten.

Paul was right. I had changed.

I'd changed the negative narrative that I lived in.

I'd changed the trajectory that was originally projected.

I'd changed expectations – mine and the Everyday Heroes who believed in me getting to this point.

I'd changed from a terrified and broken little girl, from a wounded and angry teenager, to a fear-fighting resilience ninja managing to be 10% braver and on the brink of positive disruption.

I'd started my own Shero's Journey.[10]

Mr Readman's Legacy

Without Mr Readman, there is no way I would have gone on to complete my degree and qualify as a teacher. He finished the work began by Mrs Cook and continued by Mr Williams, Mr Simpson and Miss Archer. Everything I am and everything I have is because of them and the bevy of other Everyday Heroes in my life.

Learning compassion from him – for self and others – opened the door to being truly alive and driving change rather than merely surviving. What I learned in his lectures laid the foundation for me to become a great practitioner but also laid the foundations for me to not only forgive myself but also to go on to

---

10 On my first glance of Joseph Campbell's *Hero's Journey*, I noticed that women's roles were mostly limited to that of either mothers or lovers. Seeing as I'm both of those – and sooo much more – I upgraded it to the 'Shero's Journey', as in 'She Rose', which is exactly what my Everyday Heroes laid the path for me to do! It's grown into a whole course and a retreat now. Check it out on my website: https://jazampawfarr.com/come-on-an-exclusive-retreat-with-me.

forgive my parents. To put an end to their rent-free residence in my head. A 24/7 radio station consisting solely of low-level annoying music they play while you're on hold trying to cancel your broadband. The more overwhelmed I became, the louder those voices grew in a never-ending circular prison.

Years later, I decided to visit my stepfather and my biological mother along with the man who was going to become my husband. Ed is a humble, generous, gorgeous inside-and-out, six foot two, Black man. His muscular frame and physical size make him an ideal bodyguard – which is ironic because he's such a gentle guy and I'm far more likely to get into a fight than he is.

We went to their house, but they were out. It didn't take much detective work to find them in the nearest pub. When my stepfather clocked me his face flashed anger, then, seeing who was by my side, fear. He started to get up, remonstrating that he wasn't about to 'sit here and take any crap' from me. The tiny hold I had on my emotions, facing my abuser for the first time in years, snapped. I walked up to the table he was sat at, towered over him and hissed, 'Shut up and sit down or I'll tell everyone in this pub you're a paedophile.' He went pale, glanced around nervously and collapsed back down into his seat.

As I stood there looking down at him and exuding anger, I realised I'd done exactly the opposite of what I wanted to do – I had fallen into the trap. In that moment I'd become him, and he'd become me. I was the strong powerful one and I was asserting that dominance to make him fearful. I wanted something ultimately more powerful and satisfying than revenge – I wanted freedom.

'No,' I thought to myself as I looked at what was now a weak, old man. 'You don't get to win. I am not ever going to be anything like you. You don't get to write my story. It's mine.'

Neither were interested in my forgiveness and somehow it didn't matter. My biological mother said it was her who should be forgiving me and she never would because I tried to destroy her marriage. Her words held no sting. Compassion dilutes the sting of hate and forgiveness is a powerful force that releases you from any hold the forgiv-ee has over you. For me it ushered in a new beginning and released me to build successful, fun-loving and deeply connected relationships – especially with the love of my life, Ed.

Whenever people ask me what my proudest achievement is, it's my marriage (closely followed by the three phenomenal humans produced by that marriage!). I still marvel at that little girl who once knew, beyond a shadow of a doubt, that she could trust no one, now free from doubt and fully trusting the man beside her. Ed and I are still madly in love today and are both firm believers in the fact that it's never too late to have a happy childhood.

Be Mr Readman: Reflections

1. **Eat the good, spit out the bad**

   Eating the good and spitting out the bad could be applied to education, relationships or life in general. What's worse than finding a worm in your apple? Realising you've swallowed the other half! What beliefs or assumptions or expectations have you swallowed in the past that are no longer serving you today?

2. **Evict unwelcome guests**

   If you've ever been told by someone else that you're not enough, or that you're worthless, you may have that playing on quiet repeat in your head. Like a dimmer switch, the light is on low, but it may still affect all of your thoughts, feelings, beliefs, words and actions. Just as the anger I felt towards my parents, long after I'd physically escaped them, affected my thoughts. Who do you need to deliver the line 'You've finished your bottom wash' to?[11] What are you no longer prepared to allow to occupy your mental real estate without paying rent?

3. **Be Number 73**

   Imagine a relay race where 100 runners need to run a lap and pass the baton. Only the baton is a child – a golden baton! People might stay and cheer for the first few runners and come back for the last 99 and 100 but nobody is watching number 73. In fact, they've all gone out for hot dogs or popped to the loo at that stage. But if number 73 isn't there it leaves a gap between 72 and 74. A gulf for the child to fall into. You might not be the final runner getting all the cheers, but you are an essential element in the journey. Who are you carrying the baton for, even when nobody's watching?

4. **Choose professional vulnerability and personal authenticity**

   Not the other way round! Mr Readman demonstrated the perfect balance of being comfortable without knowing all the answers and committed to finding some whilst being totally aligned with his values. Everybody wants authenticity but there's not such a big queue at the vulnerability desk. Vulnerability is the very thing that makes authenticity such a valuable

---

11 It sounds better in Twi: it's something my Ghanaian in-laws say to make it clear you're no longer being afforded favour in any way, shape or form.

currency. How's your balance? What do you have in place to look after yourself whilst also showing up as your authentic self?

5. **Opt out of the Disadvantage Olympics**

   Often I'll come off stage and people are moved and gracious enough to share their story with me. I've noticed that they often start with the phrase 'My experience wasn't as bad as yours but ...' It's not a competition and compassion isn't a limited resource! We've all experienced pain. Where might you be comparing yours to another's and minimising your own experiences? This is an invitation to stop that and lean into living a more full-fat life.

6. **Embrace the three Es: Empathy, Engage and Enrol**

   A constant frustration from the adults trying to help me was them undermining their own influence by expecting me to opt in and trust them right from the get-go. Look around: brands, charities, gangs – they employ a totally different technique, similar to my three Bs. The three Es are a surefire way of getting someone on board. It starts with *Empathy* – meeting someone where they are without judgement is a world away from sympathy, which is just feeling sorry for someone. Next step is to *Engage* in genuine conversation, doing more listening than talking, and finally *Enrol* by inviting them into a new way of thinking and being. How could your attempts at enrolling students be improved by laying the groundwork of empathy and engagement first?

7. **Create your own *Shero's Journey***

   Or He Rose or They Rose or whatever feels right for you. You are the hero in your own story – is that evident in the way you show up? Map your personal or professional journey so far and identify any spaces where you've discounted yourself. We all upgrade our phones but sometimes fail to upgrade our stories!

8. **Find more weirdos**

   Most of us have experienced being the odd one out. Identity is up to you but belonging requires agreement from the crowd. Who are your people? The ones that support but also aren't afraid to challenge you to help you grow? If you don't have any, seek them out. Maybe they haven't reached the stage in their journey that you are already at, and an invitation from you might be all they need.

9. **Practice radical re-storying**

    Restoring puts things back how they were but re-storying allows for a bit more stretch. In the past I've told many of the stories in this book with a complete lack of compassion for myself. I realised how much I still held myself accountable for what was done to me and how I had a habit of being hard on myself. Unprocessed negative narratives can leak into the way we think and feel and the things we say and do. Which of yours are you ready to re-story in your own life?

10. **Consider forgiving a*sholes**

    Whilst being sucked into a never-ending scroll of YouTube videos I found one by Nadia Bolz-Weber.[12] A six foot one inch recovering alcoholic and addict, famous for her tattoos and the founding of the House for All Saints and Sinners. In the video she lays out why forgiveness isn't about being a doormat but breaking chains. She compares forgiving to being a freedom fighter and goes on to describe how freedom fighters are dangerous because they aren't controlled by the past, or afraid to speak their truth. You know what I'm going to ask: have you banked enough compassion to forgive yourself yet?

---

12 See https://www.youtube.com/watch?v=VhmRkUtPra8.

The Power of Everyday Heroes

Statistically, I should be dead.

Or lost in a world of exploitation.

Or addicted to substances.

Or in prison.

I'm none of these things. In fact, my life is an abundance of joy, family, connection, love, hope and chocolate Hobnobs.

How did that happen? And how do we replicate my journey for children and adults suffering today?

This book has taken me years to complete. On stage I speak from a place of healed scars – not open wounds. Writing this book has, at times, required poking a particularly pointy stick into wounds I didn't know I had.

Reliving some of this – dragging hard truths from the corners of dark cellars – has been more than hard – it's been brutal. I've remembered rage, I've mourned losses, I've cried tears of sadness and gratitude. I've had to pause and place the manuscript aside for my own sanity. I've re-engaged with the deep personal work that healing requires and I've gone back into therapy – twice.

And it has all been totally worth it.

Because I'm not the hero of this story – you are.

During one particularly harrowing writing hiatus, Rachel Johnson, CEO of PiXL, invited me to speak at their Leadership Conference.[1] Rachel is all about human-first leadership and purpose driven change, also I'm a bit of a fangirl so it was an easy yes! The event was held in our nation's capital at Central Hall Westminster – a building steeped in history. The first meeting of the United Nations was held there. Giants like Winston Churchill, Martin Luther King, Gandhi and Winnie Mandela once stood on that very stage to speak.[2]

---

1   See https://www.pixl.org.uk/.
2   ... and Robbie Williams – who has also achieved a lot. He didn't quite fit into that list, but I didn't want to miss him out.

Towards back of the stage, a table had been laid for speakers and hosts. I took my place next to Rachel, waiting to deliver my keynote. As I glanced down, I caught sight of a pile of papers in front of her – printouts of that day's presentations. One page was sticking out. I recognised the image instantly and felt my breath catch.

I knew the photo, but the sight of it in such illustrious surroundings allowed me to see it in a new light. Me and four of my siblings, dressed in filthy clothes, standing outside a dilapidated house. Desperate. Poor. Neglected. The truth of our childhood frozen in time, captured in full colour.

My eyes dropped to the floorboards beneath me – the very boards where world changers had once stood – and I felt imposter syndrome engulf me.

How did I make it here?

How does a previously underestimated, neglected, abused, broken, brown, female foster kid from an under-resourced community – with more labels than a TK Maxx store – go from crouching on the steps of a rat-infested cellar to standing on this stage?

It's the question that's been lurking in between the lines of every page you've read. This book began with the death of my brother. Paul's overdose wasn't just a tragedy – it kickstarted the question. Why him? Why not me?

I've attempted to answer this as best I can. Paul and I had the same start, the same background, the same experiences, the same parents ...

But I had you.

I had Everyday Heroes who reached into the chaos to tell me that I mattered.

I had Everyday Heroes who saw past my surface to my true worth.

I had Everyday Heroes whose ordinary actions had an extraordinary impact on me.

The five Everyday Heroes I describe in my TEDx Talk and in this book didn't have today's safeguarding training or trauma-informed practice guidelines.[3] The Children's Act, giving every child the right to protection from abuse, was introduced in 1989, the year after I became an adult. Sometimes policy arrives too late for the children it was designed to protect. Often Everyday Heroes are already taking action.

---

3   You've not seen it yet? Let's remedy that now: https://www.youtube.com/watch?v=q3xoZXSW5yc.

The adults I describe in this book simply met me where I was, without waiting for me to be where the system needed me to be. They were human first, teacher second. They stood shoulder-to-shoulder in the chaotic fire of my life and refused to move, even when I pushed them away.

Mrs Cook taught me bravery through revolutionary kindness.

Mr Williams became my beacon of truth by daring to name what others ignored.

Mr Simpson showed me the power of unwavering consistency.

Miss Archer taught me audacity by refusing to let me settle for survival.

Mr Readman showed me that compassion is the key that unlocks transformation.

Because of them, I went on to fulfil Mrs Cook's vision and become a teacher. Today, I am still benefitting from the impact of those Everyday Heroes. I marvel at how much my life has changed as a result of those positive relationships.

That's the answer. The difference is you.

Any adult who is around young people has the potential to be an Everyday Hero. I don't care what your title is. You know what they say: you're defined by your soul, not your role!

Being 10% braver could be just raising your hand in a meeting. It could be starting an entire revolution or it could be leaving that toxic relationship that you know is hurting you.

Over the last thirty years, being 10% braver has led to coaching leaders, advising international governments and delivering over 3000 keynotes to over one million individuals worldwide.

As a keynote speaker I'm less interested in inspiring people and more interested in them taking action. This is why I share my story. Not for sympathy or shock value, and certainly not to get into some pointless argument on the platform formerly known as Twitter about zero tolerance and behaviour management in schools!

This is my experience. I share it because stories open doors to possibility. Whether you're an MP, a teacher, a parent, have left an abusive relationship or are navigating your own past trauma, your story is powerful – especially for those who are on the same journey as you and are stuck wondering if there is a way though. You are living proof that there is!

To all educators reading this: thank you. You already know this, but I want to say it anyway. You're doing something extraordinary every single day, even if it doesn't always feel like it.

Thank you for standing at the gate on a freezing winter morning and greeting students with warmth.

Thank you for fighting for the highest good of your students, taking the time to build a relationship, noticing and acknowledging their small victories.

Thank you for resisting the temptation of a blanket zero tolerance policy and, instead, choosing to get curious about what's behind the front, meeting students where they are and embedding a restorative approach in your school.

Your work changes lives. Literally.

Thank you for showing up as your authentic self, day after day. You're not just teaching content, you're teaching children that they matter, that they belong, that they're worth believing in.

Please invest in your greatest resource. Yourself. You know what they say on airlines: put your own oxygen mask on first ... and then pick your favourite child.[4] Schools talk a good game when it comes to mental health and wellbeing for students but aren't always great at putting their money where their mouth is.

Model celebrating your own achievements. You are a living WAGOLL![5] Failing to prioritise your own wellbeing is basically saying: 'Hey kids, work really hard, try your best, never give up, keep pushing through – no matter what – and one day you could end up just like me ... bitter, twisted, knackered and praying for early retirement.'

You don't have to fix everything. You're not Miss Honey in *Matilda*! Gathering up all the children in pain and taking them home would probably end up with you having a breakdown yourself! This isn't just a case of teacher burnout. It's a societal failure to protect those who are doing the most vital work and ties in with the shortsightedness of a quick-fix solution over the long-term cost of not investing in change early on. Remember it's value over resource. You don't have to be perfect. You just have to be consistently, authentically present in those small moments.

---

4   Or something like that. I'm paraphrasing here!
5   What A Good One Looks Like – that's you, that is!

You don't have to be a superhero. You don't have to work miracles. You just have to be the adult who sees them. Who meets them where they are. Who stands with them until they can stand alone.

This isn't about adding even more to your already ridiculous workload, it's about recognising that your most powerful tool isn't your subject knowledge or ability to 'manage behaviour' – it's your humanity.

You may never have your standing-in-Tescos-clutching-a-pork-pie moment when that child you think you failed to reach comes screeching past the frozen pizzas to tell you that you changed their life. But for that child, that name, that face you've been holding in your heart as you've read this book – you are an Everyday Hero.

That's why I wrote this book. To assert your Everyday Hero status and remind you that …

Your

Work

Changes

Lives.

The lost little girl who started writing this book, back when it was called *The Truth According to Me,* would be gobsmacked with gratitude that you've read this. She'd see it as proof that someone listened to her authentic, messy, imperfect and vulnerable truth.

I imagine her stepping out from the darkness, squinting in the light but refusing to be overwhelmed by the brightness. I imagine her seeing the line of future Everyday Heroes that would help her to stand in the light until it becomes her natural home.

That's what you did for her. For me.

It's what you continue to do.

Every day.

And your true impact is as mind-blowing as it is immeasurable.

How does a child claw her way out of the cellar, step onto the stage, heal, shine and go on to invite others to re-story their own lives?

Simple.

Because of you.

Last Words

A couple of years back, the Speaker Awards were established.[1] I went along on the night and won two awards, including the prestigious title of Speaker of the Year! If you've seen me on stage, you might have also seen the seriously unflattering photo of me taken at the exact moment my name was announced. Dumbfounded expression, mid-sob, with tears and snot cascading down my face.

What people didn't see was what happened after. Riddled with imposter syndrome I spent the next year trying to convince myself of something everyone else already seemed to know: that I was good at connection, changing hearts, moving minds and inspiring people into action.

The next year, when the Speaker Awards came around again, I attended. Only I didn't win two awards that year ... I won four! Including Speaker of the Year for a second time. I went on to be inducted into the Hall of Fame and win a third Speaker of the Year award from GTEx. There comes a point where you have to go with facts over your own feelings of self-doubt. Where you have to stop believing the lies you tell yourself and start trusting what others see in you. For me, that's been a lifelong journey.

Success is like my kids' bedrooms. Neat and insta-worthy on the outside but, open the wardrobe door and instead of school uniform, hidden sweetie wrappers and a discarded chicken nugget, a bundle of imposter syndrome tumbles out. It's probably connected to the deep lack of belonging I've felt my whole life.

I'm the result of an unplanned and accidental pregnancy. Not white enough to be white, not Black enough to be Black. Not working class enough to be considered working class anymore and yet not blending as middle class. Always somewhere in between. But what I've realised is that this in-betweenness is a superpower. It allows me to stand in the middle, between opposing sides, and tell a story that connects them both.

That realisation has been crafted largely as a result of spending the last twenty-five years with the most phenomenal human male on the planet – Ed. People are often surprised to find out we run a business together. They shouldn't be. Firstly, Ed is fantastic. Secondly, we actually use and apply the same tools we share in our keynotes, coaching and workshops. Our business, Be Human First

---
1 See https://thespeakersawards.com/.

Ltd, is a brilliant combination of our talents. I'm the WHY and Ed's the HOW. While I deliver jaw-dropping keynotes on stage, Ed works with leaders and organisations to shift culture, rehumanise systems and remind people that who people are matters just as much as what they do.

At the beginning of this year, just as I was finalising the edit of this book, another project reached completion – *Re-story Your Life*, a short documentary about my childhood, produced by filmmaker Susanna Wright at Nosco Films. The film takes you to the bridge over the M1 where I once stood. The streets I survived as a child and teen. And, most uplifting of all, to my actual primary school, where I spent time with the children who are now being transformed by the same kind of Everyday Heroes that saved me.

As if that weren't enough, just weeks later, I received two letters. The first came in a University of Hull crested envelope with official-looking print. I panicked, assuming it was a forgotten student loan demand. You know the type: 'Dear Ms Ampaw-Farr, we're delighted to inform you that you still owe us more than your car is worth. Cheers.'

I had to read it three times before the words sunk in.

'In recognition of your significant contribution to public speaking, particularly in leadership, resilience, wellbeing and diversity … the University of Hull wishes to confer upon you the Degree of Doctor of Letters, *honoris causa*.'

I'm not going to lie – I thought it was a prank. My friend Mel getting her own back for the tens of times I've successfully hacked her Facebook posting hilarious fake updates.[2] I even took a picture of the letter and asked ChatGPT if it was real. The response? 'Universities are not in the habit of mistakenly offering honorary doctorates. Congratulations, Dr Jaz!' I do find ChatGPT can be a tad sassy.

A few days later, it happened again. This time it was an email and a LinkedIn DM from Bishop Grosseteste University:

'We are writing to offer you the honorary degree of Doctor of the University in recognition of your outstanding contribution to public life and your record as a multi-award-winning inspirational speaker.'

The feelings these letters cause is what I imagine it must feel like when your parents are proud of you. Only not the steady affirmation Ed and I give to our kids, but thirty years' worth slamming into my chest like a huge oversized volleyball.

---

2   … and feel pretty proud of myself for. Zero guilt here, Mel!

In the week that followed, as the news sank in, I felt claimed. It's like I've spent my life in a railway station lost property office. Don't get me wrong – I loved it there. I built friendships, family and community. Others have joined me over the years, lost in their own ways, and we made each other feel seen.

But then one day ...

One day, someone walks into lost property, points to you, and says, 'She's mine.'

Just writing those words makes me cry.

These universities couldn't possibly have known what they were healing. They hadn't read this book. They didn't know about the little girl locked in a cellar, writing stories in the dark. They didn't see the terrified teenager erupting in school. And yet, as I finished writing this book – my story – they somehow reached across time and space and whispered, 'You always belonged here.'

Some days, when I'm struggling, I whisper that sentence to myself.

More than accolades or awards, I'm grateful for the life I have, built on a foundation gifted to me by Everyday Heroes. I am living, breathing proof of the difference a handful of teachers can make. Everything I am, everything I've achieved, and everything I will go on to create, exists because five Everyday Heroes refused to give up on me.

Now it's over to you.

Who will exist because of *you*?

Courageous Conversations

Child abuse is a topic that makes people uncomfortable. And it should. But being uncomfortable isn't an excuse for looking the other way.

I recently delivered a keynote for the Pennsylvania Family Support Alliance (PFSA) during National Child Abuse Prevention Month, and that phrase – 'abuse prevention' – really got me thinking. What exactly does prevention look like?

The PFSA's approach starts with education. Like every state in the US joining in with the annual campaign, their mission is to raise awareness about child abuse with the goal of preventing it. Through symposiums and social media (#ProtectPAKids), they hammer home the message that safeguarding isn't just for organisations or those working with children and young people – it's the responsibility of every adult in every street in every town.

In the discovery call I ask exactly how they achieved that, especially with those who had little connection to children through work or their personal life. Every year on April 2nd – National Child Abuse Prevention Day – they plant flags on the Capitol lawn. Blue flags represent reported cases of child abuse from that year. Black flags represent the children who didn't survive. In April 2024, they planted 4992 blue flags and 60 black ones.[1]

It makes for a harrowing illustration but also an invitation for change.

In the UK, our own statistics make for stark reading and demand attention.

Children navigating poverty

- 4.3 million children (30% of all children in UK) are living in relatively low-income households after housing costs.
- This figure is on the increase, up from 3.6 million in 2010/11.[2]

---

1 PA Family Support Alliance, National Child Abuse Prevention Month 2024: How PFSA Drew Awareness to #ProtectPAKids [blog] (27 April 2024). Available at: https://pafsa.org/blog/2024/national-child-abuse-prevention-month-2024-how-pfsa-drew-awareness-to-protectpakids/.

2 Child Poverty Action Group, Official child poverty statistics: 350,000 more children in poverty and numbers will rise [press release] (23 March 2023). Available at: https://cpag.org.uk/news/official-child-poverty-statistics-350000-more-children-poverty-and-numbers-will-rise.

- In proportional terms, 2022/23 saw the worst increase in absolute child poverty since 1981.[3]
- According to UNICEF, the UK saw a 20% increase in child poverty between 2012 and 2019[4] – then Covid hit.

Children navigating neglect

- Neglect is the most common form of abuse in the UK.
- Around one in ten children in the UK have been neglected.
- Children often don't recognise their experience as neglect.
- Younger children are more likely to be on protection plans with neglect with older children often going overlooked.[5]

Children navigating sexual abuse

- An estimated one in ten children in England and Wales are sexually abused before the age of 16, with approximately 500,000 children abused annually.[6]
- The majority of victims first experience abuse at primary school age.[7]
- More than two-thirds of survivors do not disclose abuse at the time, often due to fear, shame or belief they won't be believed.[8]

---

3 T. Brown, In Focus: Child poverty: Statistics, causes and the UK's policy response, *House of Lords Library* (23 April 2024). Available at: https://lordslibrary.parliament.uk/child-poverty-statistics-causes-and-the-uks-policy-response/.

4 UNICEF Innocenti – Global Office of Research and Foresight, *Innocenti Report Card 18: Child Poverty in the Midst of Wealth* (Florence: UNICEF Innocenti, 2023). Available at: https://www.unicef.org/innocenti/media/3296/file/UNICEF-Innocenti-Report-Card-18-Child-Poverty-Amidst-Wealth-2023.pdf, p. 2.

5 NSPCC, Statistics Briefing: Neglect (August 2024). Available at: https://learning.nspcc.org.uk/research-resources/statistics-briefings/child-neglect.

6 K. Karsna and P. Bromley, *Child Sexual Abuse in 2022/23: Trends in Official Data* (Barkingside: Centre of Expertise on Child Sexual Abuse, 2024). Available at: https://www.csacentre.org.uk/app/uploads/2024/02/Trends-in-Offical-Data-2022-23-FINAL.pdf, p. 12.

7 A. Jay, M. Evans, I. Frank and D. Sharpling, *The Report of the Independent Inquiry into Child Sexual Abuse* (October 2023). Available at: https://www.iicsa.org.uk/reports-recommendations/publications/inquiry/final-report.html, p. 438.

8 Jay et al., *The Report of the Independent Inquiry into Child Sexual Abuse*, p. 442.

- Over 90% of children who experienced contact sexual abuse were abused by someone they knew.[9] Nearly half of perpetrators are family members.[10]
- 41% experience academic challenges, and 53% struggle with trust and intimacy, directly affecting their ability to form stable relationships.[11]
- Over 88% of survivors report long-term impacts on mental health, with depression being the most common.[12]

And those are just the numbers we know about.

But these aren't just numbers – they're children sitting in classrooms, playing outside your house, hanging around outside random takeaways, feeling alone and in need of an Everyday Hero right now.

As a society, we still tend to see child sexual abuse in particular as some sort of unfathomable scandal that happens to those who are different to ourselves. With each new report in the media, the pattern remains the same – a trusted adult hurts a child, agencies fail to communicate, everyone is horrified. We need to push past our shock and horror and have more courageous conversations. Abuse prevails in the darkness of shame, secrets, whispers and lies.

While visiting a school in the United States, I witnessed a group of four-year-olds doing their daily affirmations:

'It's not okay for someone to hurt you.'

'It's not okay for someone to touch your private parts.'

'It's not okay for someone to make you keep a relationship secret.'

I held back the emotion that welled up in my chest. It was so simple. Equipping mini humans with the words to set themselves free. I knew instantly that if I'd had those words, if I'd known it wasn't okay, that the teachers in my school were absolutely not in agreement with my parents, I would have spoken sooner.

---

9   NSPCC, Statistics Briefing: Child Sexual Abuse (January 2025). Available at: https://learning.nspcc.org.uk/research-resources/statistics-briefings/child-sexual-abuse, p. 15.
10 Jay et al., *The Report of the Independent Inquiry into Child Sexual Abuse*, p. 440.
11 Jay et al., *The Report of the Independent Inquiry into Child Sexual Abuse*, p. 441.
12 Jay et al., *The Report of the Independent Inquiry into Child Sexual Abuse*, p. 441.

Letter to the Eight Year-Old-Me

Hello Lovely Mini Human,

You. Are. Amazing.

Yes! I'm talking to you

You're so creative. I know it feels like your curiosity is a curse right now but it's going to be a gift to so many people later.

You are such a great sister. You look after your brothers really well, even though that's not your job. You know that, don't you? Deep down, you know that what you're going through isn't right.

Isn't fair.

Isn't okay.

I'm going to be honest with you. First off, the family you idolise in the Fairy Washing Up Liquid advert isn't real. It's pretend. Even when people do have a mum and dad who love them, look after them and are the same colour as them, things aren't necessarily perfect.

Secondly, the poverty you exist in does not have to be replicated in your mind and spirit. Your past will not be the script for your future. Hold onto that. There will be times when not all grownups you meet will understand it.

My little one, know this, there is always a way through.

You're going to face things no child should. And still you'll rise. Not just for yourself, for your brothers, your sister and for millions of people around the world. Because when you speak up, others find their voice too.

So, here's your first mission:

<u>Find an adult. Tell them what's happening.</u>

They won't hear you at first because you're using fighting instead of words.

That's okay. Don't give up. Keep trying.

It will feel like there's never a good time because they are so busy.

That's okay. Don't give up. Keep trying.

And the first time you find the courage to tell an adult, they won't believe you. You'll register the disgust in their face and think it's directed at you.

That's okay. Don't give up. Keep trying.

Make them listen. Don't stop talking until you have described all of the fear you are living through. Be brave, be honest and …

Never. Give. Up.

It will feel impossible but try hard not to listen to that inner voice of fear. I know you've got this. I look at you now and I see the strength of Aslan in that tiny body.

Lift your head. Speak up.

And in the meantime, know this …

<u>I am coming for you.</u>

And I am bringing an army of sisters and brothers – strangers who become family.

We will stand beside you, until the world knows what I know right now.

You're not broken, you're the beginning of a story no one saw coming.

Your quiet voice will be Aslan's roar.

I promise you little one, your Everyday Heroes are right. You are destined for great things. And I promise – this story ends in freedom.

With love,

Your future self

(Fear Fighter, Resilience Ninja, Positive Disruptor and World-Class Reframer. Just like you.)

To the Survivor Reading These Words

I've delivered over 3000 keynotes, and it's rare if no one shares their own story of neglect or abuse with me afterwards. I've had leaders disclosing childhood trauma in tears for the first time in their life. Parents sharing their heartbreak of hearing their own child disclose abuse from another family member.

People being 10% braver.

I receive hundreds of emails, DMs and messages from people, often it's the first time they have spoken of their own past. They tell me how my words helped them to feel empowered to tell someone, start therapy and start the journey to living free of shame.

I hope the same for you.

The shame you carry is not yours. It belongs to the person who hurt you. It does not belong to you today and it never did. You did not cause the abuse. You did not deserve it. You were not responsible for it. It is not your fault.

Hear me when I confidently assure you that your past is not a script for your future. Adverse childhood experiences are not the end of your story, not even a semi-colon, let alone a full stop. Your scars are actually your superpowers.

It is never too late to speak your truth, never too late to begin healing, never too late to have a happy childhood. Find someone you trust and tell them. Claim your right to live a full-fat life free from fear, guilt and shame.

As I say in my keynotes: 'This is what it looks like on the other side of healing.'

I'm not special or unique in any way. I even have a T-shirt that says 'Awesome by choice – not by accident!' I sought out and accepted help, I updated my story. Some days I still find myself defaulting to old scripts, which is why I continue to do the work. A pivotal point was the process of ceasing to blame myself. That opened the door to me finding love, connection, truth and freedom – and it's possible for you too.

You're still here and that means there's still time.

My best,

References

Blandford, S. (2017). Born To Fail? *Social Mobility, A Working Class View* (Woodbridge: John Catt Educational).

Brown, T. (2024). In Focus: Child poverty: Statistics, causes and the UK's policy response, *House of Lords Library* (23 April). Available at: https://lordslibrary.parliament.uk/child-poverty-statistics-causes-and-the-uks-policy-response/.

Child Poverty Action Group (2023). Official child poverty statistics: 350,000 more children in poverty and numbers will rise [press release] (23 March). Available at: https://cpag.org.uk/news/official-child-poverty-statistics-350000-more-children-poverty-and-numbers-will-rise.

Felitti, V. J., Anda, R. F., Nordenberg, D., Williamson, D. F., Spitz, A. M., Edwards, V., Koss, M. P. and Marks, J. S. (1998). Relationship of Childhood Abuse and Household Dysfunction to Many of the Leading Causes of Death in Adults: The Adverse Childhood Experiences (ACE) Study, *American Journal of Preventive Medicine*, 14(4): 245–258. Available at: https://www.ajpmonline.org/article/s0749-3797(98)00017-8/pdf.

Jay, A., Evans, M., Frank I. and Sharpling, D. (2023). *The Report of the Independent Inquiry into Child Sexual Abuse* (October). Available at: https://www.iicsa.org.uk/reports-recommendations/publications/inquiry/final-report.html.

Karsna, K. and Bromley, P. (2024). *Child Sexual Abuse in 2022/23: Trends in Official Data* (Barkingside: Centre of Expertise on Child Sexual Abuse). Available at: https://www.csacentre.org.uk/app/uploads/2024/02/Trends-in-Offical-Data-2022-23-FINAL.pdf.

NSPCC (2024). Statistics Briefing: Neglect (August). Available at: https://learning.nspcc.org.uk/research-resources/statistics-briefings/child-neglect.

NSPCC (2025). Statistics Briefing: Child Sexual Abuse (January). Available at: https://learning.nspcc.org.uk/research-resources/statistics-briefings/child-sexual-abuse.

PA Family Support Alliance (2024). National Child Abuse Prevention Month 2024: How PFSA Drew Awareness to #ProtectPAKids [blog] (27 April). Available at: https://pafsa.org/blog/2024/national-child-abuse-prevention-month-2024-how-pfsa-drew-awareness-to-protectpakids/.

Timpson, E. (2019). *Timpson Review of School Exclusion* (London: Department for Education). Available at: https://assets.publishing.service.gov.uk/government/uploads/system/uploads/attachment_data/file/807862/Timpson_review.pdf.

UNICEF Innocenti – Global Office of Research and Foresight (2023). *Innocenti Report Card 18: Child Poverty in the Midst of Wealth* (Florence: UNICEF Innocenti). Available at: https://www.unicef.org/innocenti/media/3296/file/UNICEF-Innocenti-Report-Card-18-Child-Poverty-Amidst-Wealth-2023.pdf.

About the Author

Jaz Ampaw-Farr is a multi-award-winning international keynote speaker, author and global voice on leadership, resilience and rehumanising culture. Named Speaker of the Year three times and consistently ranked among the UK's top female motivational speakers, she is renowned for her transformational messaging, masterful storytelling and ability to disrupt the status quo – with powerful authenticity, humour and deeply human truth.

Jaz's TEDx Talk, 'The Power of Everyday Heroes', has inspired hundreds of thousands around the world, and her life is now the subject of a documentary being submitted to BAFTA-qualifying film festivals.

In 2025, she was awarded two honorary doctorates – one from Bishop Grosseteste University and one from the University of Hull – for her outstanding contribution to public life and her body of work. Over the last thirty years, she has advised governments in the UK and internationally on education policy, contributed to national reform initiatives and co-authored academic papers with leading university professors.

Her work spans corporate, public and third sectors – equipping people to lead with humanity, reframe adversity and create cultures rooted in authenticity, courage and compassion.

But Jaz's authority doesn't come from theory. It comes from lived experience.

Before the awards, the headlines and the stage, Jaz was a neglected and abused child – locked in a cellar, written off by society before she could write her own name. She grew up in poverty, labelled by systems that failed to see her, before her trajectory to a life of homelessness, exploitation and crime was interrupted by five everyday hero educators. This book – and her life's work – is a love letter to them, and to all who choose to be 10% braver and take a stand.

Beyond the stage, Jaz is the co-founder of Be Human First, alongside her husband Ed. Together, they run the Human First Academy, an online leadership development platform, and proudly parent three brilliant mini humans. Jaz has fronted children's TV (*Hard Spell Abbey*), performed stand-up comedy at the Edinburgh Festival, and appears on a reality TV show every twenty years (*Blind Date*, *The Apprentice* ... she's taking suggestions for the next one).

Because of You, This Is Me is not just a story of survival. It's a masterclass in transformation.

A rallying cry for rehumanising leadership. And a blueprint for your own impact roadmap.

Let's Chat

Here are the ways that you can get in touch with me – whether it's to share your thoughts after reading this book or invite me to deliver a keynote that will make people laugh, cry and leave on a high at your event.

I'm not hard to find. You can literally type 'Jaz The Apprentice' into Google and you'll find lots of videos of me crying after being fired by Lord Sugar (and underneath that some great stuff on resilience!).

Book me to speak: https://jazampawfarr.com

Book Ed to speak: https://behumanfirst.co

Join the Human Revolution: https://learn.behumanfirst.co

Social media for all offers of a lifetime supply of chocolate Hobnobs:

https://www.linkedin.com/in/jazampawfarr

https://www.instagram.com/jazampawfarr

https://www.tiktok.com/@jazampawfarr

https://www.facebook.com/groups/theimpactlounge

https://bsky.app/profile/jazampawfarr.bsky.social

https://www.youtube.com/c/JazAmpawFarr/videos